NEAL BOORTZ

THE TERRIBLE
TRUTH
ABOUT
LIBERALS

LONGSTREET PRESS

Atlanta

THE TERRIBLE
TRUTH
ABOUT
LIBERALS

Published by
LONGSTREET PRESS, INC.
2140 Newmarket Parkway
Suite 122
Marietta, GA 30067

Printed in the United States of America

1st edition 1988
Paperback edition 2001

Library of Congress Catalog Card Number: 2001091258

ISBN: 978-1-56352-685-5

Jacket and book design by Burtch Bennett Hunter

To my wife, Donna,
my soulmate and best friend;
and to our daughter, Laura,
a source of love, joy and pride.
The rest of you should be so lucky.

OK. SO WHO IS THIS NEAL BOORTZ GUY?

In the fall of 1969 Neal Boortz, quickly tiring of his jobs as a carpet installer and part-time truckloader, decided a new career path was in order. He was going nowhere, and his back was getting sore. He was also getting more than a little tired of hiding his 1967 Pinto from the repo man every night.

After hearing that WRNG (Ring Radio)'s most controversial talk show host had killed himself (No, really! A gun to the head! Bang! Thud! Dirt nap!), Boortz called the Atlanta station to offer his services as the new controversial talk show host. He had been dreaming of a job with no heavy lifting.

It was a classic case of right place, right time! Boortz pledged at least a two-week notice before any suicide attempt, and he was hired to do some fill-in work. Two weeks later he found himself the permanent host of The Neal Boortz Show. He's been at it — enraging listeners, horrifying Liberals, hiring lawyers, and terrifying managers — ever since.

Today, twenty-nine years after starting on Ring Radio,

Boortz finds himself hosting Atlanta's number 1 radio show on News Talk 750 WSB in Atlanta.

The year 1996 brought Boortz recognition from the Georgia Association of Broadcasters as Georgia's number one major market radio personality, and recognition from *Talker's Magazine* as "America's Best Male Talk Show Host." Boortz, not being of the politically correct persuasion, would be quick to point out that being the best "male" talk show host in the nation means, by default, that he was the best talk show host . . . period. He sees no sense letting Rush Limbaugh off that easily.

These accolades earned Boortz a small bonus from WSB, which he exhausted in buying an old IBM Selectric typewriter with one of those nifty little silver balls with those letters stamped all over it, on which *The Terrible Truth About Liberals* was written.

Boortz hopes to use the royalties from this book to buy another little silver ball for his Selectric.

SPECIAL NOTE TO THE READER
ON POLITICAL CORRECTNESS

There will be no attempt whatsoever in *The Terrible Truth About Liberals* at political correctness. I will, for instance, follow the time-honored custom of using "he" and "his" in reference to entities and persons of undetermined gender. I will not plug in the occasional "she" or "hers" to placate someone's tender sensibilities. If you think that this is insensitive, so be it. Grow up. The truth, which Liberals are so fond of hiding from, is insensitive. So is life. In short, this book is not for whiners or wimps.

SO JUST WHAT DO WE MEAN BY "LIBERAL"?

In the pages that follow I am going to tell you the terrible truth about Liberals. OK, Sherlock. So the book is rather small. Don't worry, you'll get what you're paying for. It's not like you spent $22.95. The book is small because it just doesn't take a lot of prose and flowery language to get my message across. Just a small measure of logic and fact will take care of things very nicely. I try to limit my use of words with multiple syllables so that Liberals won't be discouraged from picking up this book and, perhaps, learning a bit about themselves.

If I am going to detail the terrible truth about Liberals, it occurs to me that we might want to spend just a few pages defining our terms. So, just what is this person we call a "Liberal"?

You're in luck. Twenty-nine years of engaging in verbal combat and exchanging ideas with tens of thousands of people on various issues has given me the perfect perspective from which to address this troubling question.

We are dealing with modern definitions here. I am fully aware that Liberals, in a classic sense, wanted limited government and maximum personal freedom. Well, rest assured, there's nothing classical about today's Liberals. These people want limited government about as much as you and I would like to have a root canal, and their love of personal freedom certainly has its severe limitations. Your freedom to keep what you earn would be a prime example.

Likewise, when I talk about "Conservatives" I am *not* talking about the so-called Religious Right or the Christian Coalition crowd. These folks have their own agenda, and that agenda isn't particularly friendly to my basic concept of freedom. They are referred to as Conservatives primarily by people who wish to discredit Conservatives through the association.

With those ground rules established, let's get on with detailing the basic differences between Liberals and Conservatives.

This doesn't have to be heavy reading. The difference between the Left and the Right isn't really all that hard to understand! These ideas aren't going to make those of you who proudly proclaim your Liberalism happy, but it *will* make you think.

In a nutshell — here are your differences:

- 👎 LIBERALS operate from a foundation of emotion and feelings.

- 👍 CONSERVATIVES operate from a foundation of logic and facts.

🖐 LIBERALS view people in terms of their membership in groups.

👍 CONSERVATIVES view people as individuals.

🖐 LIBERALS think government made America great.

👍 CONSERVATIVES think that freedom is what made America great.

🖐 LIBERALS think that people are too damn stupid to be free.

👍 CONSERVATIVES think that people should be free.

Some of you will instantaneously recognize the basic truth of those statements; for the rest of you, we'll do some spoon-feeding.

Listen to conversations closely. When you hear Liberals talk about governmental or social issues you will hear them talk in terms of how they "feel." When you hear Conservatives discuss the same issues they will speak in terms of how they "think." Liberals love to yammer on and on about the need for compassion and empathy. They will boast of their caring attitude and the kindness they spread wherever they go.

While wallowing in all of this feel-goodism, Liberals will seldom use logical thought processes or actual empirical facts to back up their policies, not while they can gush about "feeling the pain" of the people they obsess over. I call this weeping and moaning attitude "Obsessive-Compulsive Compassion Disorder." I don't think it's treatable.

As pointed out elsewhere in this book, it is terribly easy to show the entire world what a wonderfully compassionate and caring person you are when you can show your compassion and caring attitude by spending someone else's money, and not your own. Liberals don't recognize the distinction.

If there is anything that a Liberal truly hates, it is for some evil Conservative to come waltzing right into his pity party with a discussion of some cherished Liberal concept using the cold harsh reality of fact and logic. When Conservatives step forward with the statistics and facts needed to back up their points and ideas, Liberals start throwing temper tantrums. They start screaming about "hate" and "extremism" and try to paint their Conservative tormentors as evil and mean-spirited.

This inherent inability of Liberals to deal with an issue in a logical manner will often lead to amusing, if not ridiculous, dialogues with Conservatives:

LIBERAL: *"We have to do something about hunger. You know there are studies showing that 25 percent of the children in this country go to bed hungry."*

CONSERVATIVE: *"Oh come on now. You know as well as I do that those studies were complete nonsense. All a person had to tell the surveyor was that her child said, 'Mommy, I'm hungry,' just one time during one twelve-month period to be counted in the study as 'going to bed hungry.' What child hasn't said 'I'm hungry,' more than once in the last year?"*

Oh, oh. It's on now! The Conservative has responded to the Liberal's charge with fact and some logic. The Liberal is trapped. The last thing the Liberal wants to do here is to get into a discussion over the methodology behind the study. That would involve facts and logic, not feelings and emotion. To save the day, the Liberal is going to have to respond with an emotional outburst:

LIBERAL: *"That's the trouble with you Conservatives. You're all so full of hate. You just hate children. You want children to go off somewhere and die. You're a bunch of evil right-wing extremists. You don't care about children. You want children to starve to death."*

End of conversation.

If you think facts infuriate Liberals, you ought to see what logic does to them. Many Leftists have ended up in lengthy lethargic stupors as a result of having been exposed to toxic (to Liberals) doses of logic. Some will just sit and drool. I once saw one actually pass out.

Let me give you an example.

I have used this little analogy dozens of times in conversations with my Liberal friends and listeners during discussions about welfare policy. I have never seen a Liberal handle this situation in other than an emotional manner.

The underlying discussion is whether or not it is proper for the government to take money from one person by force and then simply give that money to another person (a welfare, food stamp, or Medicaid recipient, for example) for his personal use.

To begin the discussion, I bring up the point that our government, as our Constitution says, derives its powers "from the consent of the governed." The idea here is that we cannot and should not ask the government to do anything for us that we cannot legally or morally do for ourselves.

Sounds logical, doesn't it?

With that premise in mind I build the following scenario:

You live in a triplex. You are in apartment No. 1, Johnson is in apartment No. 2, and Wilson lives in No. 3.

You discover that Wilson is ill and cannot work. He never bothered to buy a health insurance policy because he just didn't believe he would need it for quite some time. Wilson, it seems, is not good at making rational decisions. He has no savings because it was more important to use that money for bondo for his Camaro and a good Panama City Beach vacation every summer.

You believe that Wilson is about to starve to death. His electricity is going to be cut off, and he can't afford to buy his blood pressure medication. You decide to help, charitable soul that you are. You scrounge through your bank account and find $200 to help your neighbor out.

Good for you. What a guy!

A month later Wilson is still in trouble. Your $200 wasn't

enough. It turns out that he spent $20 for a case of beer and at least another $100 or so at the dog track. Things may not be all that desperate, though. One of the thirty-five Lotto tickets he bought with that carton of cigarettes might pan out.

You decide to go visit Johnson in apartment No. 2 to see if he can chip in. Johnson tells you that, while he certainly understands the seriousness of Wilson's situation, he needs his money to send his daughter to college in the fall and to pay some of his own medical bills. Besides, he's trying to save up some cash for a down payment on a house so he can get out of this weird apartment building.

You make the determination that it is far more important for Wilson to have some of Johnson's money than it is for Johnson to keep it and spend it on his daughter's education and a new home. So, here's the question:

Do you have the right to pull out a gun and point it right at the middle of Johnson's forehead? Can you use that gun to compel Johnson to hand over a few hundred dollars for Wilson's care, and then tell Johnson that you'll be back to get some more next month?

You won't run into too many people who will tell you that they have the right to take Johnson's money by force and give it to Wilson. They might say that they would try to talk Johnson into being a bit more charitable, but they don't think that they have the right to just rob him at gunpoint.

Then comes the killer question. You look at your Liberal friend and say: "Well, if our government derives its powers from the consent of the governed, how can you ask your government to do something for you that, if you did it for yourself, would be a crime? Why would it not be OK for you to take that money from Johnson by force and give it to Wilson, but it would be perfectly OK with you if the government went ahead and did it?"

At this point you sit back and watch your Liberal friend wrestle with his battle between compassion and logic. Logic will tell him that you have a definite point here. His compassion will tell him that it doesn't matter. Hand over the money.

To the Liberal, Wilson's grave situation and his need for money supersede any questions as to the morality and legality of transferring income, by force, from Johnson to Wilson.

Moving on now . . .

- 🗩 LIBERALS view people as members of groups, with group rights.

- 👍 CONSERVATIVES view people as individuals, with individual rights.

A primary distinguishing characteristic of the typical Liberal is that he has a tendency to view people not as individuals, but as members of groups. There are very few individual identities to Liberals, only group identities.

Again, all you have to do is sit back and listen. Liberals will generally talk of "the poor," "the less fortunate," "the Blacks," "the rich," "the disadvantaged," and so on. You just don't seem to have a meaningful existence to a Liberal if you can't be categorized into some group.

Not only do Liberals not think in terms of individuals, but the very word is offensive to many of them.

Several years ago a young female student served on the Diversity Committee at a northeastern state university. This student became concerned that the deliberations of the Diversity Committee did not favor the rights of individuals on campus.

This student wrote a letter to the other members of the committee telling them of her concerns for the rights of individuals on the campus and of her abiding belief in the concept of individual rights.

The letter found its way to the faculty member advising the committee. It was later returned to the offending student with several corrections, including the word "individual" being outlined in red.

Alongside the offending word the professor wrote a note telling the student that she should exercise restraint in her use of the word individual as it seems that many people consider that word to be racist.

Racist? The word individual is racist? How in the world could that word be racist?[1]

The professor went on to say that any attention or recognition paid to the individual strengthens the concept of the

---

[1] Please see the chapter on racism. You will immediately see that this professor was in dire need of emotional help from the university's psychology department.

individual over that of the group. Since the majority group in this country is white, the term "individual" strengthens the concept and image of the white majority over all others. This makes the term racist.

We immediately know a few things about this professor:
1. He's a bloomin' fool.
2. He's a Liberal.[2]
3. He wouldn't have a prayer of meaningful employment in the private sector.
4. He can't define racism.

🖐 LIBERALS think government made America great.

👍 CONSERVATIVES think that freedom is what made America great.

When was the last time you heard a Liberal speak in glowing terms of the role of freedom and liberty in the development of America and our way of life? Well, don't hold your breath. When a Liberal speaks of the greatness of America, they are speaking of the greatness of our government.

Liberals are in love with government because they are in love with power. Government gives them the ultimate power, the power to exercise control over the assets and the very lives of people whom the Liberals think are just plain too damn stupid and helpless to survive without help.

---

[2] Now I know that the first two items here, saying that the professor has been identified as a fool and a Liberal, seem to be redundant. Deal with it. They are.

Bill Clinton[3] has done a particularly good job of promoting this idea that America is great because of her government. On more than a few occasions Clinton has reminded us that he believes the role of our government is to "give people the tools they need to survive and prosper."

The tool that people need to survive and prosper in America is freedom. The freedom to interact with one another, without undue interference, for the mutual benefit of all parties concerned. This freedom is ours. It is our birthright. It is this freedom which has created, in the United States, the highest standard of living together with the greatest degree of economic independence ever enjoyed by the people of any nation.

When our immigrant ancestors came to the shores of this country they dreamed of seeing the Statue of Liberty at the end of their long ocean crossings, not the Capitol in Washington. They came here to experience our freedom . . . not to fawn over our government.

Freedom is not something that is given to us by government. We form those governments to protect the freedoms that were already ours.

Freedom, as you know, carries some pretty heavy responsibilities. To be free means that you are responsible for your life. To use force to make someone else responsible for your life is to deny that person their freedoms.

---

[3] Sorry. I just seem to have some sort of a block about referring to this man as "President" Bill Clinton. It occurs to me that the office of the presidency, which I honor, is disgraced by attaching Clinton's name to it.

Seeking the cooperation and help of others when you face a problem is one thing. Compelling another person to help is quite another. The role of government is to compel.

You will never hear a Liberal suggest that the private sector is the appropriate place to look for solutions to problems, or that an individual American just may have to bear the responsibility of some basic problem-solving themselves.

You really have to hand it to the Liberals on this one. Not only do they think that the solutions to virtually all problems flow from the government, but they have managed to get the vast majority of Americans to feel exactly the same way.

Casual observation will show you that the first place the average person looks for a solution to a problem today is the government.

"I can't afford medical insurance. The government ought to do something."

"I need more job skills to move up in this company. The government should teach me those skills."

"My boss won't give me time off to go to the dentist. There ought to be a law."

"Day care is getting too expensive. The government ought to help me pay for this."

For decades the big-government Liberals have been teaching their loyal subjects that the government is there to solve their problems. The tragic result is that now people can't imagine looking anywhere else, much less to themselves, for solutions to life's difficulties. This, of course, works out very well for the Left. When people depend on the government to solve their problems, it translates into job security, not to mention power, for those inside of government.

Your chances of having Dick Clark and Ed McMahon deliver a $10 million check to your front door after next year's Super Bowl is greater than your chances of ever hearing a Liberal suggest that the government might not have a role in solving some particular problem.

Now that you have read this, I should warn you that Liberals can become quite aroused and insulted if you ever suggest to them that government might not have a legitimate role in solving a particular problem. When you see their eyes flashing, you might want to back off. Liberals are already unstable. There's no sense in getting them any more angry than they already are.

🖒 LIBERALS think that people are too damn stupid to be free.

🖒 CONSERVATIVES think that people should be free.

This is certainly one of the more vexing traits of your average Liberal. They have an insufferable, and totally unjustified, superiority complex.

Liberals sincerely believe that the vast majority of Americans are simply too ignorant to exist on their own without the guidance and security that only a Liberal, centralized government can provide. They have absolutely no confidence in the ability of the human mind to adapt to rapidly changing economic and social circumstances and to survive.

The brutal truth is that if you took your average Liberal from the halls of some Ivy League college and plopped him down in the middle of a forest in the Pacific Northwest with nothing but a compass and a pocket knife, he would be an appetizer for a bear in just under two and one-half hours. If he lasted into the darkness of night, he would mark his shorts, if not just die of fright, the first time one of his prized spotted owls hooted at him. Take some right-wing extremist and put him out there in that same forest and by the next morning he would be warming himself before a fire on a bearskin rug in a log cabin he built overnight. The Liberal, whom the right winger will have rescued, will be outside chopping firewood for his keep.

This would be our proof that there *is* a God.

There are, to be sure, other vexing traits found in many, if not most, Liberals. For instance, Liberals seem to have a fondness for domestic animals that defecate in the house. I guess that's understandable, considering that's what they have been doing to our sense of independence for decades. Then there's that unexplainable penchant for Volvos, their love of the French language, and the tendency to wear glasses that are way too small for their heads.

So . . . at this point you are probably wondering whether I am a Liberal or a Conservative.

Neither.

I'm a Libertarian.

You aren't ready for that one yet.

WHY ARE COLLEGES AND UNIVERSITIES INFESTED WITH LIBERALS?

If you want to really go out there and find a hive of Liberals to stir up (which, by the way, can be quite a bit of fun), just visit your local college or university.

It is no secret that the halls of academia are dank havens for the Left, but you may not be entirely clear as to why.

One of the principal reasons, of course, can be found in the old adage: "Those who can, do; those who can't, teach." (To which some have added, "and those who can't teach, administrate.") But there is another theory that has been running through Internet e-mail systems that offers a more clear explanation for the persistent infestation of higher education with Liberals. I do not claim authorship. I just pass it on to you here because it makes perfect sense. Since it makes perfect sense, it's not going to rest easy with any Liberal who accidentally picks up this book. Imagine my distress.

We go back to the time of the Vietnam War. You will remember that there was a sharp division of opinions over whether or not the United States had any business being involved in the problems of Vietnam. This isn't the place to argue the pros and cons of our involvement in Vietnam.

Suffice it to say that Liberals were more likely than Conservatives to oppose that involvement. Some Liberals were so opposed that their intellectual brilliance caused them to pose, complete with hideous grins plastered across their faces, for photographs on the very anti-aircraft batteries that the enemy was using to shoot down American pilots!

As the Vietnam War heated up, more and more young men of Liberal persuasion were looking for ways to avoid the draft. Everyone knew that one of the easiest ways to avoid military service was through the student draft deferment.

As the Vietnam War dragged on, many of these Liberal antiwar protesters found their student deferments running out. Graduation could well have meant a notice from the local draft board.

The solution? Stay in school! By the tens of thousands, students extended their college careers for no other reason than to extend their student deferments. Three or four more years in a master's or doctorate program meant three or more years to hide in a classroom and wait out the end of the war.

Since these young Liberals were staying in school for the sole purpose of avoiding the draft, it hardly made sense to pursue an academically challenging course of study. Why, after all, would you need to suffer the pressures of advanced mathematics, calculus, or thermodynamics when all you want to do is keep that precious student deferment?

The answer? A liberal arts course of study. Keep it easy. Go for that master's in history, that doctorate in philosophy or government. Maybe a graduate degree in black studies would be the ticket. Perhaps English literature or political science would be the way to go. Just so you keep the deferment.

Finally, the war ended. (We lost, in case you have forgotten.) As the soldiers returned from Southeast Asia our colleges and universities were belching out hoards of relieved Liberals with their liberal arts degrees. It was a truly disgusting spectacle, not unlike that of a hyena regurgitating a tainted meal. There was a slight problem, though. Now that these Liberals were free of the threat of military service, they wanted work. The want ads are not exactly full of advertisements seeking people with advanced degrees in history, English or gender studies. So, it's back to the only place where employment opportunities really exist for them — college. This time as an instructor, soon to be an assistant professor, then a professor, then the Dean.

In short, one of the primary reasons our colleges and universities are so full of Liberals is that so many of them fled there to escape service during the Vietnam War, and couldn't escape.

They remain there to this day spreading their Liberal views to eager and impressionable young students.

Before we get into just what these Liberals have done to the young minds of today's college students, it should be pointed out that this same explanation can be applied to the current Liberal domination of journalism. Most of the biggest names in journalism today came from liberal arts colleges (Columbia comes to mind) that harbor entire herds of Vietnam era Leftists who found their vocations while hiding from the draft.

It's an interesting exercise to walk into a freshman journalism class and ask these youngsters why they have chosen to study journalism. "Because I want to change the world" would be your typical reply.

A diligent professor, free of the shackles of mindless Liberal ideology, would tell these students that it is not the job of a journalist to save the world. The job of a journalist is to gather and report — in as interesting, accurate, and informative a manner as possible — the salient facts concerning a particular news story. Sure, tell that to a fresh-faced young news producer at a major network who is determined to rid the world of evil and make it a better place!

There is just one more thing that needs to be added about the media. I have worked with these people for almost thirty years. Believe me, I'm not just making things up here. From the youngest news writer to the most experienced reporter or anchor, these people are absolutely and completely convinced of one fact — that they are smarter than the average American and that all of us would certainly perish if it were not for the superior wisdom that is handed down in daily radio, newspaper, magazine, and television doses.

To be completely fair here, it should be noted that more Americans get their news from TV tabloid shows such as *Hard Copy* and *Inside Edition* than they do from network newscasts or newspapers.

Could someone please give me a few good reasons why we should have confidence, let alone a modicum of hope, about the future of America when people who can vote are getting their daily dose of news from *Hard Copy*?

Maybe these journalists, even with their insufferable superiority complexes, have a point.

THE COLLEGE YEARS: BLUDGEONING YOUNG MINDS

Now that you understand just why our colleges and universities are havens for Liberals, you need to consider the effect these Leftists have on the young, impressionable minds entrusted to their care.

Day after day, college students are subjected to a seemingly endless procession of Liberal college professors who, as you now know, couldn't possibly find meaningful employment in the private sector. These students are programmed with the liberal, big-government, forced-compassion ideology these professors acquired in the '60s, and they are taught that anyone who does not agree with these ideals is either evil, insensitive, extremist, ignorant, hate-filled, or all of the above.

So, what do these young minds get out of college? Well, in addition to a sprinkling of basic knowledge that just might, with a little bit of luck and knowing the right person, come in handy in their chosen fields, they spend four torturous years or so learning (just for starters):

1. That it is better to "feel" and to "care" than to "think" and to "reason."

2. That those who succeed in life do so through "luck." These people are "fortunate." Hard work and good decision making have absolutely nothing to do with their success.

3. That those who have failed in life did so because they were the "less fortunate." They just weren't lucky enough. Golly, it just wasn't their day.

4. That one person's failure constitutes a lien on another person's hard work and success.

5. That income is distributed, not earned.

6. That when anything bad ever happens to any member of an officially recognized minority group, it is because of either racism or sexism.

7. That the Left is good, and the Right is evil.

8. That private businesses are the causes of the problems of society, and that more government is the only solution.

9. That we really have no need for a military anymore, except to deliver flour, bottled water, and corn dogs to refugees.

10. That taxes in the United States are way too low, and, besides, the rich certainly don't pay their "fair share."

11. That their parents are hopeless reactionary tools of the corporate structure.

12. That anyone who has more than they have got that way through greed.

13. That Bill Clinton is actually to be admired.

To make matters worse, today's college graduates have probably heard (or will hear) some more of the same nonsense during their graduation ceremonies!

For years I have been lamenting the fact that I have never been invited to deliver a commencement address at a college or university. Little did I know that there was some obscure federal law which stated that any college or university which dared to have a Conservative deliver a commencement speech would lose all federal grant money and student loan funds.

In 1996 I learned that an amphibian, Kermit the Frog, actually delivered a commencement speech. Enough! The last straw!

I decided not to wait for an invitation (that was obviously never coming) from some graduating class. On June 6, 1996, I delivered my own commencement speech to my alert and attentive listeners on News Talk 750 WSB in Atlanta.

After the speech was delivered on my radio show, I started fielding thousands (well, hundreds . . . maybe a dozen) of requests for tapes or transcripts. (OK! Seven people asked for a copy!) A recording of the speech also became available on my "Best of Boortz '96" compact disc in December 1996. The first printing of the CD sold out in less than twenty-four hours. The second printing lasted a few days longer before they were gone. Each printing consisted of a dozen CDs.

Now, in the next chapter of this beautifully bound book, you are going to read "The Commencement Speech," slightly embellished.

The terrible truth is that this is a speech that would never be tolerated at most colleges or universities. If, through some type of subterfuge, I ever was afforded the opportunity to deliver this speech to a graduating class, I can guarantee that it would be the last time. These people communicate with one another, you know.

It might be a good idea, therefore, for you to rush out and buy a second copy of this book (Lord knows I could use the extra twenty-eight cents) to send to your favorite new college graduate. This is the commencement speech they'll never get to hear.

THE NEAL BOORTZ COMMENCEMENT SPEECH

---

*We operate on the assumption at the beginning of this stirring
address that a gracious introduction of Mr. Boortz has been
delivered by a very junior member of the faculty who
owed a lot of people a lot of favors. As Boortz
takes to the podium, one or two
people actually clap!*

Thank you so much for that most gracious introduction.
Would you mind if I asked where you got that gaudy robe?

I am honored by the invitation to address you on this
august occasion. It's about time. Be warned, however, that I
am not here to impress you; you'll have enough smoke
blown at you today. And you can bet your tassels I'm not
here to impress the faculty and administration.

After I say what I came to say, there will be precious little
chance I will be invited back here to deliver another address.
Not here, not anywhere. This is my one chance for a commencement address. In short order, you will know why.

You may not like much of what I have to say, and that's
fine. You will remember it, though. Especially after about

ten years out there in the real world. This does not apply to those of you who will seek your careers and your fortunes as government employees. Those of you who have the mentality to become a career government employee will probably never understand what I am about to say.

This gowned gaggle behind me is your faculty. You've heard the old saying that those who can, do; those who can't, teach. That sounds deliciously insensitive. But there is often raw truth in insensitivity, just as you often find feel-good falsehoods and lies in expressions of compassion. Say goodbye to your faculty now, because you are getting ready to go out there and do. These folks behind me are going to stay right here and teach.

By the way, just because you are leaving this place with a diploma doesn't mean the learning is over. When an FAA flight examiner handed me my private pilot's license many years ago, he said, "Here, this is your ticket to learn." The same can be said for your diploma. Believe me, the learning has just begun. You ain't seen nuthin' yet.

Now, I realize that most of you consider yourselves Liberals. In fact, you are probably very proud of your Liberal views. You care so much. You feel so much. You want to help so much. After all, you are such a compassionate and caring person. Hey, that's fine! Now, at this age, it's as good a time as any to be a Liberal, as good a time as any to think that you know absolutely everything.

You have plenty of time, starting tomorrow, for the truth to set in.

Over the next few years, as you begin to feel the cold breath of reality down your neck, things will change. You will change. If not you, certainly that person next to you.

So here are the first assignments for your initial class in reality: Pay attention to the news, read newspapers, and listen to the words and phrases that proud Liberals use to promote their causes; then compare these to the words and phrases you hear from those evil, heartless, greedy, extremist, and hate-filled Conservatives.

From the Left you will hear "I feel." From the Right you will hear "I think." From the Left you will hear references to groups — the Blacks, the Poor, the Rich, the Disadvantaged, the Less Fortunate. From the Right you will hear references to Individuals. On the Left we hear talk of group rights; on the Right, individual rights.

That about sums it up, really: Liberals feel. Liberals care. They are pack animals whose identity is tied up in group dynamics. Conservatives think. And, setting aside the theocracy crowd, their identity is centered on the individual.

Liberals feel that the masses, their favored groups, have enforceable rights to the property and services of productive individuals. Conservatives (and Libertarians, myself among them, I might add) think that individuals have the right to protect their lives and their property from the plunder of the masses.

In college you have worked very hard to develop a group identity — Go Panthers! Go Warthogs! Go Tri-Delt, or whatever Greek alphabet soup you have been simmering in.

These diplomas, though, have your individual names on them. Not your school mascot, not the name of your fraternity or sorority, but *your* name. Your *individual* identity starts now. You're on your own.

If, by the time you reach the age of thirty, you do not consider yourself to be a Libertarian or a Conservative, rush right back here as quickly as you can and apply for a faculty position. These people will welcome you with open arms. They will welcome you, that is, so long as you haven't developed an individual identity. You will have to be willing to sign on to the group mentality once again.

Now, I'm not talking in the abstract. I've been there, done that. I was one of you. During my college years at Texas A&M, I was a lot further to the left than you are now. I joined the Students for a Democratic Society, carried signs, occupied the university president's house (well, his front porch anyway). I was cool. I was happening. I was aware. I cared. I was tuned in. I felt. I obsessed. I followed. I was a complete waste. I did everything but think!

What happened, you ask? I got a job! Thinking about it now, maybe I should say we got a job. You see, after I got out of college I found out that I had a lifelong partner that was intent on sharing every productive thing I did. That partner was, in some ways, an agent. An agent representing a strange and diverse group of people.

An agent for every teenager with an illegitimate child.

An agent for every malcontent who wanted someone else to provide them with a place to live.

An agent for a research scientist who wanted to make some cash answering the age-old question of why monkeys grind their teeth.

An agent for some poor demented slob who considered himself to be a meaningful and talented artist, but who somehow couldn't manage to sell his artwork on the open free market.

An agent for every person with limited, if any, job skills . . . but who wanted a job at City Hall.

An agent for tin-horn dictators in fancy military uniforms.

An agent for multimillion-dollar companies who wanted someone else to pay for their overseas advertising.

An agent for everybody who wanted to use the unimaginable power this agent has for their personal enrichment and benefit.

That agent is our wonderful, caring, compassionate, oppressive government.

I was petrified at the unimaginable power this agent has. Power that I didn't have. A power that no individual has, or will have. This agent has the legal power to use force. The power to use a gun to accomplish its goals.

I did not necessarily choose this partner in my work life and personal life. The government just walked up, introduced itself rather gruffly, handed me a few forms to fill out, and moved right on in. It slept anywhere it wanted to.

And let me tell you, this agent is not cheap. It takes about 40 percent of everything I earn. Actually, the way this agent looks at it, it takes 100 percent of everything I earn and then lets me have about 60 percent of it back. That 60 percent is carried as an "expenditure" on my agent's books.

I can't fire this agent, and I can't lower his commission on my work. He has that power, not me. I don't trust my agent, and I don't particularly like him.

Be clear on this: It is not wrong to distrust government. It is not wrong to fear government. In certain cases, it is not even wrong to despise government. In fact, it may well be praiseworthy. A praiseworthy American tradition.

Government is inherently evil. There's no question it's a necessary evil. After all, we do need some structure to settle disputes between us and to defend against foreign and domestic aggressors. But, like some drugs that in the proper dosage can save your life, an overdose of government can make you very ill indeed, or it could even be fatal.

Let's address a few things that have been crammed into your minds at this university. There are some ideas you need to expunge as soon as possible. These ideas may work well in an academic environment, but they fail miserably out there in the real world.

We'll talk first about diversity. Diversity is a new favorite buzz word of the Left and of academia. Look around. As soon as the word "diversity" came over the PA system you probably saw one or two of your professors actually swoon! I can hear some of them breathing heavily from here.

Diversity! Diversity! Look at your faculty! The ecstasy on their faces! Diversity! I'd better stop. This could get messy.

You have been taught that the real value of any group of people — be it a social group, an employee group, a management group, or whatever — is based on diversity. This is a favorite Liberal ideal because diversity is based not on an individual's abilities or character, but on a person's identity and status as a member of a group. There we go with that left-wing group dynamics thing again. With diversity the group identification — be it racial, gender- based, or some other minority status — means more than the individual's qualifications.

Well, you are about to move from this atmosphere where diversity (whatever that *really* is) counts, to a workplace and a culture where individual achievement and excellence count. No matter what these mental zombies behind me have taught you for the last four years, you are about to learn that diversity is absolutely no replacement for excellence, ability, and individual hard work.

Believe this. From now on it's your individual identity and your individual achievements that count. The importance of your group identity will fade.

Next, let's address this thing you seem to have about "rights." We have witnessed an obscene explosion of so-called "rights" in the last few decades, mostly emanating from college campuses.

You know the mantra: You have the right to a job. The right to a place to live. The right to a living wage. The right to health care. The right to an education. You probably even have your own pet right — the right to a Beemer, for instance, or the right to have someone else provide for that child you plan on downloading in a year or so. Well, hold that pet "right" up there in front of you now. Visualize it! Feel it! I want you to be consumed by your newfound "right" as you hear these next words.

Forget it!

You have absolutely no right to anything. You have no right to anything that demands that another person surrender either his time or his property to you for the fulfillment of your right.

You cannot receive health care unless some doctor or health practitioner surrenders some of his time — his life — to you. He may be willing to do this for compensation, but that's his choice. You have no "right" to his time or property. You have no right to his life.

You think you have some "right" to a job — a job with a living wage, whatever that is. Do you mean to tell me that you have a right to force your services on another person, and then the right to demand that this person compensate you with money? Sorry, forget it. Just how would you react if some urban outdoorsmen (that would be "homeless person" for those of you who don't want to give these less fortunate people a romantic and adventurous title) presented his smelly self to you and demanded his job and your money?

The people who have been telling you about all the rights you have are simply exercising one of theirs — the right to be an imbecile. Their being imbeciles didn't cost anyone else either property or time. It's their right, and they exercise it brilliantly.

By the way, did you catch my use of the phrase "less fortunate" a bit ago? When I was talking about the urban outdoorsmen? That phrase is a favorite of the Left. Think about it, and you'll understand why.

To imply that one person is homeless, destitute, dirty, drunk, spaced out on drugs, unemployable, and generally miserable because he is "less fortunate" is to imply that a successful person — one with a job, a home, and a future — is in that position because he is "fortunate."

The dictionary says that fortunate means "having derived good from an unexpected place." There is nothing unexpected about deriving good from hard work. There is also nothing unexpected about deriving misery from choosing drugs, alcohol, and the street.

If the Left can create the common perception that success and failure are simple matters of "fortune" or "luck," then it is easy to promote and justify their various income redistribution schemes. After all, we are just evening out the odds a little bit.

This "success equals luck" idea the Liberals like to push is seen everywhere. Remember Democratic Representative Dick Gephardt's reference to high-income earners as "people who have won life's lottery"? You got it! They are making the big bucks because they were — all together now — lucky!

It's not luck, my friends. It's proper choices and hard work.

One of the greatest lessons I ever learned was in a book by Og Mandino, entitled *The Greatest Secret in the World*. The lesson? Very simple, really: "Use wisely your power of choice."

That bum sitting on a heating grate, smelling like a wharf, is there by choice. He is there because of the sum total of the choices he has made in his life. This truism is absolutely the hardest thing for some people to accept, especially those who consider themselves to be victims of something or other — victims of discrimination, bad luck, the system, capitalism, whatever. After all, nobody really wants to accept the blame for his position in life. Not when it is so much easier to point and say, "Look! He did this to me!" than it is to look into a mirror and say, "You S.O.B.! You did this to me!"

The key to accepting responsibility for your life is to accept the fact that your choices, every one of them, are leading you inexorably to either success or failure, however you define those terms.

Some of the choices are obvious: Whether or not to stay in school. Whether or not to get pregnant. Whether or not to hit the bottle. Whether or not to keep this job you hate until you get another better-paying job. Whether or not to save some of your money, or get that new car.

Some of the choices are seemingly insignificant: Whom to go to the movies with. Whose car to ride home in. Whether to watch the tube tonight, or read a book on investing.

But, and you can be sure of this, each choice counts. Each choice is a building block — some large, some small. But each one is a part of the structure.

If you make the right choices, or if you make more right

choices than wrong ones, something absolutely terrible may happen to you. Something unthinkable. You, my friend, could become one of the hated, the evil, the ugly, the feared, the filthy, the successful, the rich. Quite a few people have made that mistake.

The rich basically serve two purposes in this country.

First, they provide the investments, the investment capital, and the brains for the formation of new businesses. Businesses that hire people. Businesses that send millions of paychecks home each week to the un-rich.

Second, the rich are a wonderful object of ridicule, distrust, and hatred. Nothing is more valuable to a politician than the envy most Americans feel for people with more than they.

Envy is a powerful emotion. Envy can be even more powerful than the emotional minefield that surrounds Bill Clinton when he greets a new covey of White House interns.

Politicians use envy to get votes and power. And they keep that power by promising the envious that the envied will be punished: "The rich will pay their fair share of taxes, if I have anything to do with it."

The truth is that the top 10 percent of income earners in this country pay a ridiculous amount of all income taxes collected (see chapter entitled "Who Really Pays the Taxes"). I shudder to think what these job producers would be paying if our tax system were any more "fair."

You have heard, no doubt, that in America the rich get richer and the poor get poorer. Bull! That statement is provably false. The government's own numbers show that the poor actually get richer, and the rich, in large numbers, get poorer.

Let's assume, though, that this "rich get richer" bit is true. For some of the rich, it is true. Why? Because they keep doing the things that made them rich in the first place. Ditto for the poor. The rich keep saving their dollar bills, while the poor keep spending theirs.

Speaking of the poor, you should know that under our government's definition of "poor," you can have a $5 million net worth, a $300,000 home and a new $90,000 Mercedes (completely paid for), a maid, cook, and valet, and $1 million in your checking account, and you can still be officially defined by our government as "living in poverty." Now there's something you haven't seen on the evening news.

How does the government pull this one off? Very simple, really. To determine whether or not some poor soul is "living in poverty," the government measures one thing. Just one thing. Cash income. It doesn't matter one bit how much you have, how much you own, how many cars you drive or how big they are, whether or not your pool is heated, whether you spend the winters in Aspen and the summers in the Bahamas, or how much is in your savings account. It only matters how much income you claim in that particular year. This means that if you take a one-year leave of absence from your high-paying job and decide to live off the money in your savings and checking accounts while you write the next great American novel, the government says you are "living in poverty."

This isn't exactly what you had in mind when you heard these gloomy statistics, is it?

Do you need more convincing? Try this. The government's own statistics show that people who are said to be "living in poverty" spend more than $1.70 for each dollar of income they claim. Something is a bit fishy here. Just remember all this the next time Dan Rather puffs up and tells you about some hideous new poverty statistics.

Why has the government concocted this phony poverty scam? Because the government needs an excuse to grow, to expand its social welfare programs, which translates into an expansion of its power. If the government can convince you that the number of "poor" is increasing, it will have all the excuse it needs to sway an electorate suffering from the advanced stages of Obsessive-Compulsive Compassion Disorder.

I'm about to be stoned by the faculty here. They've already changed their minds about that honorary degree I was going to get. Sure, Kermit got one, but I'm not holding my breath.

That's OK, though. I still have my Ph.D. in Insensitivity from the Neal Boortz Institute for Insensitivity Training. I learned that, in short, sensitivity sucks. It's a trap. Think about it — the truth knows no sensitivity. Life can be insensitive. Wallow too much in sensitivity and you can't deal with life, or the truth.

Get over it.

Now, before the dean has me shackled and hauled off, I have a few random thoughts.

- You need to register to vote, unless you are on welfare. If you are living off the efforts of others, please do us the favor of sitting down and shutting up until you are on your own again.

- When you do vote, your votes for the House and the Senate are more important than your vote for president. The House controls the purse strings, so concentrate your awareness there.

- Liars cannot be trusted, even when the liar is the president of the United States. If someone can't deal honestly with you, send them packing.

- Don't bow to the temptation to use the government as an instrument of plunder. If it is wrong for you to take money from someone else who earned it, to take their money by force for your own needs, then it is certainly just as wrong for you to demand that the government step forward and do this dirty work for you.

- Don't look in other people's pockets. You have no business there. What they earn is theirs. What you earn is yours. Keep it that way. Nobody owes you anything, except to respect your privacy and leave you the hell alone.

- Speaking of earning, the revered forty-hour work week is for losers. Forty hours should be considered the minimum, not the maximum. You don't see highly successful people clocking out of the office every afternoon at five. The losers are the ones caught up in that afternoon rush hour. The winners drive home in the dark. Free speech is meant to protect unpopular speech. Popular speech, by definition, needs no protection.

- Finally (and aren't you glad to hear that word), as Og Mandino wrote,

1. Proclaim your rarity. Each of you is a rare and unique human being.

2. Use wisely your power of choice.

3. Go the extra mile . . . drive home in the dark.

   Oh, and put off buying a television set as long as you can.
   Now, if you have any idea at all what's good for you, you will get the hell out of here and never come back. Class dismissed.

WHAT'S ALL THIS ABOUT A DEMOCRACY?

In this chapter I want to challenge an insidious idea that has made its way into the minds of, I dare say, the vast majority of Americans. It's an idea that was planted there by the Left, by Liberals anxious to expand the role of government and their own power. I'm referring to the idea that this country was designed as, and is supposed to be, a democracy.

Throughout your lifetime you have continually heard the United States referred to as a *democracy*. And during this time I'm sure you have heard the idea of democracy presented in nothing but the most favorable and glowing terms.

I am sure that you are absolutely convinced that the United States is a democracy. I am just as certain that you believe this is exactly what was intended by the people who founded this country.

Stand by for a surprise: You're wrong.

The word *democracy* does not appear anywhere in the Declaration of Independence. The word *democracy* does not appear anywhere in our Constitution, nor does it appear in any of the constitutions of the fifty states. That's rather odd, don't you think? Considering the widely held perception that we are, in fact, a democracy.

More surprises: Our Founding Fathers — people with names like Thomas Jefferson, John Jay, Benjamin Franklin, Alexander Hamilton, and Thomas Paine — did not think of the idea of a democracy in very positive terms at all. In fact, they had some quite nasty things to say about the concept.

You will also be surprised to know that it was the official policy of the government of the United States, right up until the 1930s, to teach the soldiers of the U.S. armed forces that a democracy was a dangerous and undesirable form of government that would lead to mob rule and the end of private property rights.

Try this: Find a copy — one published in the 1930s — of the *U.S. Army Field Training Manual.* In that manual you will find certain political definitions that soldiers were required to learn. Among those was the word *democracy.* Believe me, this official government definition of democracy was not at all complimentary. The soldiers were told that democracy means mob rule, and that it leads to a destruction of property rights. They had it exactly right.

Something changed, though. Oddly, the change happened around the time of FDR. Until the late '30s the "D" word was seldom uttered by presidents. You need proof? Go back and read some State of the Union Speeches.

Over the past sixty years, we have come to believe that the United States was formed as a democracy, that it is supposed to be a democracy, and that democracy is the way to go when it comes to governments. In this day and age you are hard-pressed to find one citizen, let alone an elected representative, who understands that the United States was not designed to be a democracy.

OK. You're probably just a bit confused here. This democracy idea has been pounded into your head for quite some time now, and it's hard to consider, let alone accept, the idea that there actually may be something wrong with the concept.

About 230 years ago a professor named Alexander Tyler had a thing or two to say about democracies. This was at a time when the thirteen original colonies were still under British control. Since the United States didn't then exist, Tyler was hardly writing about our own government. Instead, he was writing about the fall of the Athenian Republic nearly 2,000 years earlier. Little did Professor Tyler realize how his words would apply to the United States more than 200 years later.

Professor Tyler's observations are quite sobering:

A Democracy cannot exist as a permanent form of government. It can exist only until the voters discover that they can vote themselves largesse[4] from the public treasury. From that moment on, the majority always votes for the candidates promising the most benefits from the public treasury, with the result that a Democracy always collapses over loose fiscal policy, always followed by a Dictatorship.

---

[4] Largesse. What a wonderful word. Look it up, it will do you good. They are.

The average age of the world's greatest civilizations has been 200 years. These nations have progressed through this sequence: From bondage to spiritual faith; from spiritual faith to great courage; from courage to liberty; from liberty to abundance; from abundance to selfishness; from selfishness to complacency; from complacency to apathy; from apathy to dependency; from dependency back into bondage.

I think we're somewhere around the complacency/apathy part of this progression right now. We damn sure aren't anywhere close to that "courage" part.

Even the most intellectually challenged reader can see Professor Tyler's predictions coming true in this country right now.

Have we, in fact, discovered that we can vote ourselves goodies from the public treasury? Are you kidding? Just what does a Liberal politician do when he wants to make his Conservative opponent sound like the lead character in a Stephen King novel? It's easy! Just say that the evil, hate-filled, greedy Conservatives want to do away with Social Security and Medicare. These two programs are brilliant examples of people using the ballot box to stuff their pockets. These programs are sacred! They are both going to go flat broke, but politicians appear to be helpless to do anything about it because they know the voters will not tolerate even a mere hint that their access to the public treasury might, in some way, be curtailed!

So, if we're not a democracy, just what are we?

Good question, and there's a good answer: We are a "constitutional republic."

So, what's the difference?

Don't go running to a current dictionary to check the definitions of these words. The definition you would find for *democracy* will be quite a bit different from the definition of thirty or forty years ago.

A democracy is, simply put, a system where the majority rules. Whatever the majority wants, the majority gets.

"OK," you say, "so the majority rules in a democracy. How is that different from what we do? We have elections, and the person with the most votes wins. Isn't that a democracy?"

Not exactly. In the United States there are some very specific rules (the Constitution) that must be followed by everybody. It doesn't matter whether you're a sheep-dipper in Utah or a senator in Washington, these constitutional rules apply to you.

The basic rules, of course, deal with our rights to our lives, our liberty, and our property.

Under our Constitution you cannot be deprived of your life, liberty, or property just because the majority of people think it might be a good idea. The whim of the majority is reigned in by the law. If we were a true democracy, the majority could get together and decide that your home should be taken away, given to the "less fortunate," and you should be killed. "But wait!" you protest. "I haven't done anything! I have a right to my property! You can't take this without due process!" Sorry, pal. This is a democracy. You only have one vote, and that's not enough. The majority rules. Pack your bags.

There is an excellent example in our recent history to illustrate the basic difference between a democracy and a constitutional republic.

In the South, prior to the Civil Rights movement and the 1964 Civil Rights Act, democracy was the rule. The majority of people were white, and the white majority had little or no respect for any rights which the black minority had relative to property, or even to their own lives. The majority — the mob — ruled.

Then along came some people who believed that the rights of black Americans to control their lives, their property, and their basic freedom should be protected — and were, in fact, protected — by our Constitution against the wishes of the white Southern majority.

The people of the United States came to the realization that, in the South, the white majority did *not* rule. The law, not the people, was supreme. Blacks had rights under our Constitution, regardless of the will of the majority.

Democracy was out, the will of the white majority was ignored, and the rule of law was back in.

To put it in even more basic terms, a lynch mob is a democracy. There are fifty-one people there. Fifty of those people think that the remaining person should swing from an oak tree. Person Number fifty-one doesn't think a whole hell of a lot of the idea, but he's in the minority. The majority wins. The mob rules. Number fifty-one swings.

We can make this simpler still: A democracy is three wolves and one sheep voting on what's for dinner.

Don't get me wrong. I'm not bashing democratic processes. In our country we make certain decisions — such as the election of our representatives, bond issues, and other matters — based on a vote. The side that gets the most votes wins. But these democratic processes cannot, and should not, be used to deprive people of their basic rights.

So, why all this democracy-bashing? Why is all of this so important?

If you check our history, you will find that liberal politicians became fond of referring to the United States as a democracy just about the same time they became fond of the idea of big government and redistributing wealth.

Liberal politicians recognized that they could become more and more powerful if they had more government goodies to hand out. All you had to do was to make a good number of voters dependent on government hand-outs, and those voters would become absolutely loyal to whatever politician they believed would keep the government goodies coming. In short, these Leftist politicians recognized the truth in that old saying, "He who robs Peter to pay Paul can always count on the support of Paul."

Liberals knew that the government could not give away anything unless it first took that thing from whoever earned it or owned it. However, to take that thing (hard-earned money, for instance) from the person who earned or produced it without just compensation would be a violation of that person's right to his property.

The solution? Hell, let's just call ourselves a democracy! Let's promote the idea of majority rule — a rule of people instead of a rule of law. That way, when we take someone's property to give to someone else, we can say that what we are doing is really OK because it's what the majority of the people want. And, after all, we're a democracy, aren't we? Hey! It's for the common good.

When you think about it, it really doesn't appear to be too tough to get a majority of the people to approve some Liberal scheme whereby the government will take property away from the wealthiest 30 percent of the people in this country and distribute it to the remaining 70 percent. It all sounds like a great idea to those on the receiving end. It's not all that great a concept to the 30 percent who are getting ripped off, but, hell, we're a democracy! The majority rules! That's what democracies do!

Let's not belabor the point. My goal here is a simple one. I know that this little book isn't going to start a movement whereby the concept of democracy receives the discredit it so richly deserves. The best I can hope for is to have this idea of mob rule — a lynch mob or a gang of looters — flash through your mind every time you hear a politician speak of our "democracy." Maybe you'll also wonder, for a second or two, if that politician truly knows what he's talking about.

Those of you who become convinced, through your own thought processes and research, of the dangers of a democracy might be compelled to challenge the next person you hear use that word. Especially if that person is a teacher, a politician, or someone in a comparable position of authority. Just ask him, "Excuse me. No disrespect intended, sir, but what makes you think our country is a democracy, or that it was even supposed to be a democracy? I've looked, and I can't find the word anywhere in our Declaration of Independence or Constitution."

You, like me, will get to the point where you just love to watch those people squirm.

Remember, lynch mobs are democracies. Maybe you'll think we deserve something better.

BUSINESSES DON'T PAY TAXES

OK. So that last chapter was just a bit long. The individual chapters start to get a bit shorter now. Why?

Because it just doesn't take all that many words to debunk cherished Liberal myths. We'll start here with the idea that businesses and corporations pay taxes.

Haven't you heard Liberal politicians talk about businesses needing to carry more of the tax burden? You probably think that's a good idea, don't you? After all, those huge, rich, evil multinational corporations should pay more taxes so that the little people can keep more of their own money to spend.

If those thoughts have seriously crossed your mind then you have fallen victim to a massive Liberal con job.

For starters, consider these points:

1. There is absolutely no limit at all to the government's desire for your money. Liberal politicians want as much of your money as they can possibly get their hands on, and they will keep reaching into your pocket and grabbing your cash right up to the point where they start to

seriously fear you are about to cut their hands off.

2. These liberal politicians will use any subterfuge, any lie, any trick they can to keep you from realizing just how much the government is really costing you.

An example: During Bill Clinton's 1998 State of the Union speech he bragged that America had the smallest government in decades. The Liberals in the House Chamber dutifully applauded this lie. Then Clinton went on to propose a federal budget that would consume 20.1 percent of the Gross Domestic Product, the total value of all goods and services produced in the United States during that year. Not once since the end of World War II had our government consumed that much of the GDP.

Just how, dear attentive reader, do you square Clinton's claim to the smallest government in decades with the reality of his budget proposal?

Let's go back to businesses supposedly paying taxes.

When politicians think they have pushed the individual taxpayers to the breaking point, they will start to talk about raising taxes on businesses and those evil corporations.

Washington politicians, especially the Liberal ones, believe that the average American actually thinks that businesses and corporations pay taxes. Unfortunately, sadly, these people are right; the average American thinks just that.

But the average American is dead wrong.

Here is a lesson that Liberals do *not* want you to learn.

They know it's true, but they don't want you to find out. The following paragraph is pornography to a Liberal.

The *only* entity in this country that pays taxes is the individual! Corporations and businesses do not pay taxes. They collect taxes from individuals and pass them on to the government.

Virtually every economist in this country who is not working for the government[5] will concur with this statement.

On second thought, maybe I had better expand on that. Let's try again: Virtually every economist in this country who is not working for the government or teaching in a college or university will concur with this statement.

When a business or corporation takes money out of corporate earnings to send off to the government in the form of taxes, that money isn't created out of thin air. If the money had not been paid to the government as taxes, it clearly would have been used for some other purpose. The money could have been used to pay salaries, give employees raises, pay stockholder dividends, pay profits to owners, buy raw materials, have a company barbecue, put new leather upholstery in the corporate jet . . . you get the general idea. Sending that money to Washington means it isn't going to be spent by that company somewhere else.

Now, if the money paid to the government was going to

---

[5] An important distinction. Government economists are being paid to preach the government mantra. They shoot straight with you on this and they are suddenly looking for jobs in the (ugh) private sector.

be used for salaries, just where did that money actually come from? Those dollars came right out of the pockets of the employees who would have received a raise or of the new employees who would have been hired.

OK, so what if no raises or new hiring were in the picture? Then the money might have been paid to stockholders as dividends, or to the owners as profit. Either way, when the money is diverted to taxes, it has to come out of the pocket of some individual — the individual stockholder or the owner.

Whenever a dollar is spent, it eventually filters down to an individual somewhere. The person who provided the beef or the plastic forks for the employee barbecue. The worker who built the stomach pump used on half the staff the night of the company barbecue. The man who stitched the new leather upholstery in the business jet. Or the farmer who raised the cow that gave up its life for the cause of hamburgers and comfortable corporate posteriors.

Our economy operates for the benefit of individuals. All profits and earnings are eventually spent to benefit individuals, and all costs of doing business are eventually paid by individuals.

The individual is the basic unit of our economy. This is where all bucks stop.

So, when a corporation pays a dollar in taxes, that dollar ultimately comes from some individual's pocket.

When taxes are raised on corporations or businesses, those taxes are paid by individuals somewhere. The employee who goes without the raise. The person who doesn't get hired. The stockholder who sees his dividend decrease. The farmer who can't get a good price for his cow.

Somewhere an individual human being pays. The business or corporation collects the money, and off it goes to Washington.

So, when you hear some Liberal yammering about the need to raise taxes on businessmen and rich corporations, that politician is talking about raising your taxes.

Just for the hell of it, you should drop him a line and let him know that you're on to him.

WHO REALLY PAYS THE TAXES?

Now that you understand that all taxes end up being paid by individuals, just who are the individuals paying most of the taxes?

When Bill Clinton was running for president the first time, he talked about his plan to raise taxes on the "rich" so that they would be paying "their fair share." This liberal mantra proved to be extremely popular with both the voters and most of the talking heads in the media.

Clinton and his liberal supporters also loved to refer to the 1980s as the "decade of greed." This painted a picture of evil, greedy, rich people lining their pockets during the '80s while the rest of the poor, oppressed Americans picked up the load on income taxes and saw their fortunes dwindle.

Hey! It all worked. This all added up to a spectacular election victory.

This picture of greed and the evil lifestyle of the rich has been a mainstay of Liberal thought and rhetoric for decades. Liberals know that one of the most powerful of human emotions is envy, and they know that it is perfectly normal to be envious of those who have more than you do.

Well, here's the antidote for this anti-achievement

Leftist venom you've been fed. If, after you read this, you still believe that the rich aren't paying their fair share, and that they were the only ones to benefit during the economic expansion of the '80s, then you are indeed a lost soul.

Liberals know that bashing the rich works. It gets votes. It works because of two factors: ignorance and envy. This "pay their fair share" and "decade of greed" nonsense certainly sounds great to people who don't have the slightest clue of who is paying what in income taxes. It also appeals to those who cannot contain their jealousy and envy for those who have more than they do.

Before you read any further, try this little test. Believe me, the remainder of this chapter will mean so much more to you if you will just play along for a second.

There are two blanks for you to fill in below. In the first blank I want you to pencil in the percentage of total income taxes collected by the federal government in 1997 that you think are paid by those people in the top 1 percent of all income earners. In the second blank I want you to pencil in the percentage of total income taxes you think are paid by the top 10 percent of all income earners.

Give it a shot.

_____% Percentage of all federal income taxes collected which were paid by the top 1 percent of income earners.

_____% Percentage of all federal income taxes collected which were paid by the top 10 percent of income earners.

My guess is that you were off. Way off. You are probably in another galaxy. In fact, I would go so far as to say that if you were anywhere close to the actual figure, it is only because you are one of those mindless people who listens to those hate-filled radio talk show hosts.

The actual figures? Since the Internal Revenue Service has not yet issued its reports on the 1997 tax year, these are estimates. The numbers are extrapolated from 1995 and 1996 statistics.

The top 1 percent of all income earners in the United States earn about 14 percent of all of the income. They pay about 30 percent of all of the income taxes collected.

Are you believing this? The top 1 percent pays almost 30 percent of all income taxes paid in this country! And they earn only 14 percent of the income!

Moving on. The top 10 percent of the income earners earn a little more than 40 percent of all income, but they pay nearly 70 percent of all income taxes collected.

Just a little amazed, aren't you? Just 10 percent of the income earners in this country paying almost 70 percent of the taxes! Wow!

But, wait a minute. Maybe they sweetened their deal during those horrible greed-filled Reagan years. That's it! These robber barons used to pay more, and now they're paying less.

Sorry. Doesn't wash. At the beginning of 1983, when all of the nice Reagan tax cuts were taking place, the top 1 percent was paying just 20.3 percent of the taxes and the top

10 percent was paying 49.7 percent. The share of the income taxes the rich paid during the "decade of greed"[6] actually went up!

Now, that should take care of the "not paying their fair share" idea. The higher income earners are obviously paying a much higher share of the income taxes than those in the middle or lower income groups.

What about this "decade of greed" idea that Clinton, his myrmidons[7] in the media, and other Liberals have been pushing as a label for the Reagan years? As the numbers have shown, there was no need for some knight in shining armor to come sleazing out of Arkansas and punish these evil rich people for the hideous tax breaks they got during the '80s.

From 1983 to 1993, the percentage share of the total income taxes collected by the U.S. government went up not only for all taxpayers in the top 1 percent and the top 10 percent, but also for those in the top 25 percent and the top 50 percent. It went down (from 7.2 percent to 4.8 percent) only for the bottom 50 percent of all income earners.

By any measure this does not reflect greed, nor does it support the idea that the rich are not paying their fair share.

---

[6]Greed, by the way, is a word that is impossible to accurately define. Suffice it to say that it is a word of art used by Liberals to implant horns on the foreheads of achievers.

---

[7]Now here is a wonderful word. Myrmidon. If any word accurately describes the average democratic voter, this would be it. Look it up. I'm not going to do all of your work for a mere $12.95.

So, were these figures available to Clinton when he was talking up his famous 1993 increase? The one that he said would make rich people pay their "fair share"? You bet they were. He knew the facts. The media knew the facts. But the facts didn't matter. Clinton was playing the numbers, the election numbers, and the game was working too well for anyone (in the media, for instance) to come along and douse the fire.

I don't want this to be a civics class, but a brief lesson in the numbers of elections will help you to understand why liberal politicians are always so quick to propose tax increases for the rich and tax cuts for the middle class.

When you propose a big tax increase on the nasty, filthy rich, you know that you are making points with about 90 percent of the voters. Sure, the high income earners aren't exactly toasting you at dinner, but they have only about 10 percent of the votes, so . . . big deal. They probably weren't going to vote for you anyway. So, what have you got to lose? Nail 'em, and watch the votes from the other 90 percent pour in.

If you propose a tax decrease on the middle class . . . no problem! The middle class loves it, and they will have more money to spend that will benefit the businesses that are, more likely than not, owned or serviced by those nasty rich people.

Politicians want to stay in power. To do that they need votes. The surest way to get the largest number of votes is to buy them. To get the money you need to buy these votes you take it away from the people whose votes you do not need . . . and you give that money to, or spend that money on goodies for, the people with the votes you do need.

It's all so simple.

No wonder the rich are paying such a huge proportion of the taxes. Liberals need their money, but they don't need their votes. The lower income people have the votes but not the money. Guess who gets nailed.

Now, hopefully, you will never again be able to listen to Liberals whine about the rich not paying their fair share of taxes without rolling your eyes.

GROUND RUSH

In the next two chapters we are going to deal with a cherished Liberal program . . . one of the greatest vote-buying schemes of all time. Social Security. When you finish reading these chapters you should be ready to grab pitchforks and shovels and march on Washington.

Hold on now, all you young readers. I know that as soon as you read the words Social Security your immediate thought was to put down this book and pick up something more interesting. Almost any of the junk mail you received today will do. You think this topic is excruciatingly boring. Only blue-hairs and wizened, toothless old men are worried about Social Security.

Well, you don't have blue hair and you aren't sure what wizened means, so this isn't for you. You sit there smugly thinking that you are far too young to be worried about Social Security.

So let me tell you about "ground rush."

It's a skydiving term. When you go through training to jump out of perfectly serviceable airplanes, you learn about ground rush . . . and you learn how it can kill you flat dead.

Just a few seconds after jumping out of an airplane, you will be falling at about 120 miles per hour. Here's the strange part: You don't really believe you are falling! You think that you must be caught in some type of updraft. You just aren't getting any closer to the ground. Or so you think.

Skydivers learn to recognize this little mind trick and to guard against it. They know that as they near the ground it will suddenly — very suddenly — appear as if the ground is rushing up to meet them at a terrific speed. If they haven't pulled the rip cord and deployed their parachute, it may be just a tad late. The consequences aren't very pretty and can take a long time to clean up.

You may have experienced a variation of ground rush on expressways. That bridge way down the road doesn't look like it's getting any closer. Suddenly it rushes toward you and disappears quickly behind you. Bridge rush.

At work you've probably experienced deadline rush. That project deadline seemed so far away, so you delayed working on the project (pulling the rip cord). Suddenly that deadline came screaming across the calendar, and you found you didn't have time to do the wonderful job you honestly intended to do.

So why is ground rush important to you?

Because somewhere out there, down the road a bit, is that time of your life called "retirement." Right now retirement seems so far away that you can't really conceive of ever getting there. You're not really falling. The ground isn't really getting any closer.

Just as the ground will seemingly accelerate toward the skydiver, or the bridge to the driver, or the project deadline to the unwary employee, so will your eventual retirement suddenly appear down the road, rushing toward you with blinding speed.

Time accelerates. You won't believe how fast.

If you don't already have your parachute open, it's going to be quite an impact.

Over the next few years there will be much debate in Washington on what to do about Social Security. You will be affected, strongly affected, by what happens in that debate, so you had damned well better pay close attention.

The Social Security debate — it's not just for geezers anymore. So read, now, about Social Security and how the Liberals are sabotaging your best chance for a comfortable retirement with deficit spending.

It's later than you think.

YOUR PAYCHECK:
YOUR EMPLOYER
"CONTRIBUTES" NOTHING!

You had better start thinking about retirement sooner, rather than later, or your "golden" years are going to be spent scratching yourself while sitting on the crude wooden deck you built outside your double-wide and watching your neighbor tinker with his rusted-out Camaro.

You need to understand this right now: Social Security isn't going to cut it. You would be better off depending on a lottery ticket to provide you with a comfortable retirement.

The fact is that the main purpose of Social Security is *not* to provide you with a basic retirement income. The main purpose of Social Security is to redistribute wealth, to make an increasingly large number of Americans dependent on government for their basic needs in their retirement years. As you know, this dependency is easily exploited for votes.

When a Liberal Democrat finds himself in the last days of a campaign, with the polls showing a possible narrow loss, all that Liberal has to do is charge that his opponent wants to do away with Social Security. This tried and true practice of Liberal politicians is always good for a kick in the polls and thousands of extra votes.

The Social Security system is broke, folks. The way the law stands now, you are going to pay far more into Social Security than you could ever hope to take out. Unless, that is, you manage to qualify for Social Security disability payments right off the bat by, say, getting maimed as an innocent bystander accidentally caught between Bill Clinton and a campaign donation.

If a private company was running this Social Security scam on the American people, its officers and employees would all be arrested and charged with heinous crimes against humanity. Social Security isn't being run by a private company, though. It's being run by politicians and protected by Liberals.

There is a push to reform the Social Security system. The push is coming generally from Conservatives. The resistance to change is coming from the Left. If these Liberals would let you take all of that money you are going to flush into the Social Security system and instead invest it in stocks and bonds (real big "if" here), you would end up with five to ten times more retirement income. That could be the difference between your double-wide in East Podunk and a condo on the beach at West Palm.

As soon as you started your first job the liberal protectors of this grand income redistribution scheme started working one of their slickest scams on you: You were told that your employer is going to "match" your Social Security "contribution."

Two things: First, it isn't a "contribution"; it's a tax. Contributions are voluntary; Social Security taxes are not. Second, your employer isn't matching anything. Every single penny paid to Social Security on your account is coming straight out of your pocket.

We're going to do something a bit foreign to the Liberal mind here. We're going to use some logic.

When an employer makes a decision to hire you, he budgets a certain amount for your employment. That amount is based on several considerations, including the prevailing market wages for your particular job skills, how much money he has available, and your expected economic value to his business.

To illustrate: Let's say your employer determines that he can budget $50,000 for the cost of your employment. Does that mean that you are going to be paid $50,000 a year? Hardly.

Think about it this way. If you determine that you have $600 a month to set aside for the expenses associated with automobile ownership, are you going to go out and buy a car that has monthly payments of $600? Not if your IQ exceeds room temperature.

If you blow your entire automobile budget on payments, where are the insurance payments going to come from? What about gas? Maintenance? Tires? That pesky yearly license tag? You had better leave room in the budget for those goodies.

Well, your employer has to leave room in his budget for

the various costs associated with putting you on his payroll. This is all going to come out of the $50,000 a year he has budgeted for the cost of your employment.

Just a partial list of the costs of your employment includes unemployment insurance, worker's compensation insurance, health benefits, paid vacations, parking, even the cost of the coffee you get from the employee's coffee cave every morning. Believe me, it adds up.

Oh . . . and one more thing. That so-called "matching contribution" to your Social Security tax has to come out of the budget, too.

When all is said and cried over, your employer may have about $42,000 left from the $50,000 he budgeted to put you on the payroll. Guess what — *that's* your salary.

This nonsense of splitting up your Social Security tax into your "share" and your employer's "share" is a blatant scam set up by Liberals to keep you from realizing the true cost of this absurd income redistribution program. They know full well that if you realized what it was costing you, they would have a bit of a nasty little taxpayer revolt on their hands.

It's your money. All of it. And you'll be damned lucky to ever see it again.

Every time that money disappears from your paycheck, spend a few moments thinking of how you could be investing those dollars for your own retirement.

Angry? You haven't even *started* to get angry yet. Read on.

IT'S JOB SECURITY FOR LIBERALS AND A POOR RETIREMENT FOR YOU

After reading the last chapter you now understand that the total amount paid to the Social Security scheme under your name — both the amount taken directly out of your paycheck and the amount the government is trying to con you into believing was "contributed" by your employer — comes directly out of your pocket. You paid it. All of it.

There are no virgins paying Social Security taxes.

A young person just getting out of college today has approximately forty-five years to work. This person will be retiring in about the year 2042. What this person may not know is that the year 2042 is about thirteen years after the Social Security system is scheduled to go broke. You read right — thirteen years!

Did you catch that word? Broke. No money. The system into which you will have paid thousands of dollars a year will be broke! Bankrupt!

If we can count on history as a guide to the future, the Liberal protectors of Social Security will try to solve this problem by (1) increasing the retirement age to seventy-five or so, in hopes that the system will be saved because so many people will take the dirt nap before they can qualify for benefits, or (2) by raising Social Security taxes another couple of percentage points to put off the inevitable bankruptcy.

Oh, I almost forgot. They are also considering a system whereby you don't get any Social Security benefits at all if you lived your life responsibly enough that you can provide for yourself after retirement. You still pay the taxes. You just don't get the benefits unless you can prove that you need them.

Isn't your government wonderful? Believe me, it gets worse. There is a little situation that evolved in Southeast Texas that Liberals would just as soon you don't know about.

About fifteen years ago our federal government made a bit of a mistake. It allowed some local governments around the country to pull their employees out of the Social Security system. Many governments and government agencies took the hint and ran like hell.

Some local governments that opted out of the Social Security scheme allowed their employees to do their own retirement planning. Others instituted pension, retirement, and other plans that did not mirror Social Security at all.

But three Texas counties did something unique when they pulled their employees out of Social Security. They continued to require those employees to pay exactly the same amount into a retirement/disability plan as they were previously paying to Social Security. The counties also "matched" those payments, just as your employer would. This means, just as with Social Security, that the entire amount was effectively being paid by the employee.

OK, so how did the employees in these three counties do? Let's use Galveston County, Texas, as the example.[8]

These figures you are about to read are so spectacular I wouldn't blame you if you thought I was feeding you a big one. This time I'll tell you where I got them. They came from Brief Analysis No. 215 of the National Center for Policy Analysis in Washington, DC. I'm not sure, but I think these people analyze government policies.

Galveston County employees voted to get out of the Social Security system in 1981. Each employee's new contribution to the retirement system was 13.78 percent, very close to the old Social Security contribution. Of that amount, 9.737 percent was paid into each employee's private individual retirement account, which returned 6.5 percent, compounded daily. The remainder was used to pay disability and life insurance premiums to cover employees in case of an accident or premature arrival at room temperature.

I know, numbers can be dry and boring. Well, the results of Galveston County's retirement plan are anything but dry and boring. Wait till you see what happens to Galveston County employees when they reach retirement age.

First example — a county employee on the low end of the scale, making about $20,000 a year. If this person were to rely on Social Security, he would be getting the princely sum of $775 per month. Wow! What a deal! Just where is

---

[8] The other two counties involved were Brazoria and Matagorda.

he ever going to spend all of that money?

This county employee is lucky, though, because he has the Galveston County Alternate Plan. Instead of $775 per month, he gets $2,740 a month. Quite a difference! Think, for a moment, of what this could mean to your own retirement plans.

What about higher-paid county employees — the professional types, engineers, administrators, etc.? A Galveston County employee who was making about $50,000 a year would get about $1,302 per month from Social Security. That's about $15,600 a year. But (oh happy day!) he doesn't have to rely on Social Security. The Galveston County Alternate Plan is going to pay him $6,843 a month. That's $82,000 a year compared to $15,600!

There's more.

Under Social Security, when a worker dies there is a one-time death benefit paid to his survivors — the princely sum of $255. Under the Galveston plan that worker's survivors get a life insurance payment equal to three times his salary. The minimum is $50,000 with a $150,000 maximum.

By any measure, the employees of Galveston County, Texas, have a much better retirement deal than the millions of Americans who must rely on Social Security. Let this sink in . . . Galveston County employees get fatter checks after they retire than they did when they worked. Do you think you will fare as well under Social Security?

So, if such tremendous benefits can accrue outside of the Social Security system, why haven't more governments bailed out like Galveston County did? They didn't because they couldn't. In 1983, Liberals in Congress passed a law saying that nobody else could escape. They erected an economic Berlin Wall between you and a comfortable retirement. It was a matter of survival. Too many people stood to escape government dependence for independence. Independent people don't vote for Liberals.

If you aren't yet convinced that Social Security is a bad deal, and getting worse, maybe this will do it.

In 1950, when your parents might have been starting grade school, there were sixteen people working and paying their Social Security taxes for every person receiving benefits.

In 1997, there were about 3.3 people working and paying Social Security taxes for every person on the taking end. By the year 2030, the ratio will be less than two to one.

Think of it this way: It's one thing when one hundred people go together to buy a yacht, but if ninety-eight of them die and leave the remaining two with the full cost of yacht ownership, you're going to see a "for sale" sign real quick, or an insurance claim.

It's plainly obvious. Social Security is a disaster. So, you are probably wondering, why isn't it being fixed?

Let's see how clear I can make this.

The largest single identifiable bloc of voters in this country is Social Security recipients. These are the people who drive the impossibly large cars right down the center of the busiest street in town — at twenty miles per hour with the turn signal stuck on — on the third day of every month, on the way to deposit their Social Security checks. They are the sole remaining support for the white cotton glove industry.

If you don't know anything else about these people, you had better believe that they vote! They vote on basically two issues — Social Security and Medicare. They couldn't care less about term limits, balanced budgets, human rights in China, family-leave laws, EPA cleanup sites, Clinton's affairs, or nuclear nonproliferation. They care about Social Security and Medicare. They care about those checks. Beyond that, they have no use for politicians.

This is nirvana for liberal politicians. They have an extremely large bloc of voters who have their votes clearly for sale to the senator or representative who will make them feel the most secure about their Social Security and Medicare payments.

Do you really think these politicians are going to care one bit that people are being ripped off by this system? First of all, they are fairly certain that you don't have a clue what is going on. Second, they know that your kind doesn't vote. At least you don't vote in numbers anywhere near big enough to offset the blue-hairs.

Bottom line: These Liberal congressmen and senators are taking your money, by legal force, and using that money to buy votes from Seasoned Citizens who won't be around to tsk-tsk when you discover that there isn't actually a Social Security account in your name, and that you aren't going to collect a thing.

Wait! You say that there is a Social Security trust fund out there and that's where all your Social Security taxes are going?

Sorry. You've been lied to again. Yes, there is a Social Security trust fund. But there is no money in that fund. Nothing. Just a bunch of IOUs from the federal government.

I'll explain the situation with an anology.

You have a very rich grandmother. When you were born, your rich grandmother promised to send your parents a check for $1,000 every year on your birthday. Your parents were supposed to take that money and invest it for your college education.

Hot dog! Your college costs are taken care of! What more could a newborn infant want?

It turns out, though, that your parents lack basic financial discipline. Every year they seem to spend a bit more than they earn. So, when your birthday rolls around every year they take Grandma's $1,000 check and use it to pay off some bills. They write a little $1,000 IOU and put it in an envelope for you.

By the time you are ready to begin your college education you discover that your college fund consists of nothing but eighteen $1,000 IOUs from your parents. What's more, they still are living beyond their means, and they just can't afford to pay off any of their debt to you. You're on your own. Tough luck.

This is precisely what the federal government has been doing with the so-called Social Security trust fund for decades. There is no money there. Just IOUs. Right now there is no problem because enough money is coming into the system in Social Security taxes every year to handle all of the benefits. In a few years, when expenditures exceed revenues, someone is going to go calling on Uncle Sam with a few IOUs. Any idea where the money will come from?

There are various Social Security privatization plans being discussed right now. This is going to be a very hot issue over the next few years.

Liberals are poised to fight. They *have* to fight! If people are allowed to take that money that they are throwing away on Social Security and invest it in the market, these people will arrive at their retirement years completely independent. Liberals know that you cannot stampede a financially independent person to the polls with dark suggestions that evil Conservatives want to reduce their Social Security benefits. If Liberals want to continue to use the Social Security system as a massive vote-buying scheme, they must avoid privatization. Independent people have this nasty little habit of voting Conservative.

Oh, and by the way . . . when you hear about plans to allow the government, rather than the individual, to take Social Security funds and invest them in the stock market to pay future benefits, that's tantamount to partial government ownership of private business. And that, by definition, is socialism.

Just thought I'd point that little goodie out to you.

ABOUT RACE

You can't escape it. America seems to be consumed with the issue of race. And there definitely *is* a race problem in this country. You need look no further than the reactions we saw from different racial groups when the infamous O.J. Simpson "not guilty" verdict was announced.

Just imagine, for a moment, the tremendous things that could be accomplished by all of the people of this country if we could stop moaning and gnashing our teeth over racial and cultural differences and interact harmoniously with each other.

Frankly, though, I'm not fully convinced that Liberals really want to see our racial divisions healed. Somehow this racial division has become a potent weapon in the hands of the Left. The conventional wisdom, nurtured by Liberals, seems to be that Conservatives are generally racist, while Liberals are essentially colorblind. This is why so many black Americans eagerly identify themselves as Liberals. Why, after all, would they want to be associated with a bunch of hate-filled racists?

Clearly, it is vitally important to the cause of freedom

and the future of our Republic that our racial differences be worked through and solved.

Hopefully you have learned by now that the first step in solving any problem is (duh!) *identifying* the problem. If you spend a few hundred dollars working on your car's engine, only to find out that the problem was with the transmission, you would feel quite stupid . . . as well you should.

Identify the problem!

The same rule applies to solving our race "problem."

Is it racism? Maybe not! Maybe it's prejudice! It could be bigotry! Maybe even culturalism! All four are different problems, and all four beg for different solutions.

Nothing I have to say is going to solve our problem of race, but I will make you this one promise: After you have read this chapter, a little bell is going to go off somewhere between your ears every time you hear anyone use the word *racism*. You will also find that you use that word a bit less often yourself.

Fact: Fewer than one in one hundred people who use the words *racist* or *racism* would be able to accurately define them.

Do you think you can define racism? Give it a try. Turn your eyes and do it now.

You're wrong. I'd bet on it.

Until recently, almost any dictionary you picked up would have a definition of racism that read something like this:

> **Racism.** *n. 1. A belief in the inherent, genetic superiority of one race of people over another and a belief in the right*

of the superior group to dominate that racial group believed to be inferior.

The key to any legitimate definition of racism is that the racist group or individual believes that it, or he, is genetically superior to another group of people.

You can dislike someone, or some group, without feeling that you are inherently or genetically superior to them. You can distrust them, fear them, scorn them, run from them, avoid them, tell nasty jokes about them, all without adopting a belief in your supposed genetic superiority . . . all without being racist.

So, why is all this so important?

If you want solutions, first identify the problem!

Most of the differences that divide blacks and whites in America are based on culture, not genetics or skin color.

A white woman is sitting in her car at a stoplight. She sees a young black male approaching. She hits that little button that locks all of the car doors. The young black man hears the thunk and says to himself, "Racist."

Did that woman lock those doors because she believed in the inherent, genetic superiority of whites over blacks? Hardly. It's more likely that she locked her doors because she was aware that a disproportionate number of young black males commit violent crimes. She doesn't believe that this crime rate exists in young black males because of their skin color. Instead, she suspects it probably has something to do with the cultural influences on them while they were growing up.

Another example: Let's say that I own a hardware store, and I'm looking for help. Two young men answer my want ad. One young man, who happens to be white, shows up neatly dressed. He carries himself well and has a good command of the English language. The other young man, black, shows up with baggy shorts worn ten inches below his navel and high-top tennis shoes with laces flopping all over the place. His baseball cap is on backwards,[9] the price tag is still attached, and he has absolutely no communications skills.

Surprise, surprise, surprise: I hire the young white guy. The young black man is absolutely convinced that he didn't get the job because he was black. He didn't get the job because I am a racist.

Is that why I didn't hire the black man? Was it because I believed that the white applicant was genetically superior to the black applicant? Or was it because I made a judgment, based on attitude and appearance, that the young white man would make a better employee than the black man?

It really isn't difficult to understand why some people are so eager to blame each and every speed bump on their road to success on racism.

If you're in a minority and you don't get a job you want, it is not only easier, but also more emotionally comfortable,

---

[9] It is a proven scientific fact that a person's IQ drops immediately by more than ten points as soon as that person puts on a baseball cap backwards. If you don't believe it, just sit somewhere and watch the behavior of people who are wearing their baseball caps this way.

to blame it on racism. If you aren't getting these jobs because of your skin color, then there's really nothing you can do about it.

But if you didn't have a different skin pigmentation to fall back on as an excuse, you might have to consider other reasons why you didn't get the job. Maybe you didn't have the necessary skills. Maybe you have a slovenly appearance. Maybe you can't communicate effectively. Maybe you don't have the right job experience.

Gee . . . maybe it's *you* and not your color!

Do you realize just what that means? It means that you have to clean up! You might have to buy some clothes that fit correctly. You might have to get some job experience before you apply for the better jobs. You might have to return to school to learn some of those things that were being taught back when you thought learning wasn't "cool" enough for you. All of these things take time. They take work. They make *you* responsible for your destiny!

What a burden. At this point you're not at all sure you want to be responsible for your own destiny. What if you fail? What if you don't make it? Who are you going to blame it on? Failure would be so embarrassing, and you would have to take the responsibility. Man, it sure was easier just to blame it on racism.

Certainly there are true racists out there, but I have never met a person who actually believed in the genetic superiority of one race over another who gave any evidence of an IQ approaching that of a slug.

Just look at these people marching around in their white robes! The greatest cultural event most bona fide racists have been to is a tractor pull. They are hideous cretins and, thankfully, few and far between.

Let's just try to be more careful about throwing around the "R" word. When you let a person use racism as an excuse for every personal tragedy, failure, and problem that comes along, then you are aiding and abetting that person in his quest to hide from reality and to avoid the responsibility that he has for his own life and his own success.

If you want to see friends succeed, and you know that they must alter some elements of their behavior to achieve their goals, you are doing them no favors if you accept their excuses for their poor behavior. If a black acquaintance tells you that he didn't get a particular job because he was discriminated against, and you suspect that the true reason for his rejection rested more on attitude than on skin color, you do him no favors with your silence.

Let's get on with solving the problems we face . . . together.

THE LIBERAL WAR ON THE INDIVIDUAL

In another chapter you learned that Liberals have this pathetic little habit of dealing with people as members of groups, rather than as individuals. Why, after all, do you think these people are called "collectivists"?

The truth is that there is a declared war going on in this country against the concept of the individual.

Our friends on the Left come by this anti-individual mentality honestly. Some of the greatest Leftists of our time have expressed thoughts that can't be considered too friendly to the sovereignty of the individual.

Here's a nice little quote for you. See if you can recognize the historical figure who uttered these words:

"Comrades! We must abolish the cult of the individual decisively, once and for all."

Maybe it would help some of the older readers if you were to imagine this person pounding his left shoe (it would have to be his left shoe, wouldn't it?) into a table as he spoke.

You're right. This statement in condemnation of the concept of the individual was uttered by none other than

Soviet Premier Nikita Khrushchev on February 25, 1956, speaking to the Twentieth Congress of the Communist Party.

I'm not trying to bury you in quotations here. I beg your forbearance for just one more. You need to realize the degree to which the Left fears the concept of the individual.

In *The Philosophy of Fascism*, written in 1936, Mario Palmeiri writes, "Fascist ethics begin . . . with the acknowledgment that it is not the individual who confers a meaning upon society, but it is, instead, the existence of a human society which determines the human character of the individual. According to Fascism, a true, a great spiritual life cannot take place unless the State has risen to a position of pre-eminence in the world of man. The curtailment of liberty thus becomes justified at once, and this need of rising the State to its rightful position."

Don't give me that "oh, but he was writing about Fascism! That's right wing, not left wing!" nonsense. Fascism is merely socialism light. It is a system of private ownership of the means of production, with government control. The German fascists of World War II were self-proclaimed big-government socialists. Does that sound right wing to you?

One of the great Liberal success stories of the past fifty years has been their ability to take the left-wing, big-government policies of Fascism and Hitler's Germany and portray them as right wing or Conservative in nature. The Liberals have used this ploy to take one of the most hated figures in the history of the world and tie him to the coat-tails of their ideological enemies. Give them credit. It was pretty slick, and it has worked beautifully.

The scale from right to left runs from limited government to a totalitarian government. Fascism is further down that road than is capitalism and free enterprise. End of argument.

At any rate, you can see that Liberals seem to have some deep, historical problem with individualism. It's no wonder. Individuals, and all the baggage that comes with them, pose, at best, a number of pesky little problems for the Left, and at worst, a direct threat to core Liberal ideals.

If, for instance, you recognize people as individuals rather than as mere components of some group, you then have to accept the fact that they have individual rights. From that point it's a greased slide to the idea that this individual might even have a right to the money that he earns and the property that he acquires with that money!

Once you have recognized the existence of the individual, and the fact that the individual has rights, then you have to consider just how those rights are to be protected! This leads you into uncomfortable discussions and arguments on the rights of the individual vs. the rights of the group — the rights of society.

As soon as that discussion is joined, the helpless Liberal will almost certainly be reminded of the "fact" ("Damn," says the Liberal, "Not another fact!") that our Constitution and our Bill of Rights grant no rights whatsoever to any groups. All rights are conferred on individuals. There is an individual, not a group, right to freedom of speech. Ditto for freedom of religion.

Liberals love to talk about the rights that certain groups have. Blacks and Hispanics, for instance, have a right to a proportional representation in the workplace, thus the need for affirmative action. Conservatives will counter with an argument that individual members of those groups have the right to compete, one-on-one, with other individuals for a job, a raise, or a promotion, and to be judged on those individual merits rather than their group identity.

We can use the so-called "health care crisis" to illustrate just how dangerous individualism is to Liberalism.

For decades the principal Liberal fantasy in this country, other than redistributing income, has been the establishment of a system of nationalized health care. It makes sense — for Liberals. If you are in love with big government, and if you believe that America is great because of government, then what better way to show your love of government than to take about 17 percent of our economy and place it under government control. Liberals also know that once the people acquire their "right" to health care, they will be careful to vote for the politicians who protect that newfound right. Perhaps we can go so far as to say that having the control over someone's health care is tantamount to having them by the proverbial "short hairs." As we all know, give those short hairs a tug and that person's heart and mind will follow wherever you go, and that includes right to the ballot box.

To promote its socialized medicine agenda, the Left has been quite fond of talking about our "right" to health care. The propaganda campaign has worked. I dare say that a poll would show that most Americans think that such a right exists.

The "right to health care" concept is somewhat easier to push in the concept of society as a whole. The Liberals can speak of the need for society to take care of all of its members by providing basic health services so that everybody will be healthy and prepared to do his part, as a member of society, for the common good.

This grand plan for socialized medicine (and most other big-government spending programs) can be sidetracked, or even derailed, if the concept of the individual, and that individual's rights, is introduced.

Here's how.

If you argue that we have a right to health care, then it follows that someone is under a legal or moral obligation to provide that health care to us. This cannot be done unless someone gives up time (in the form of a consultation or the performance of a surgical procedure, for instance) or property (in the form of drugs, supplies, equipment, and materials).

Here is where those troublesome individual rights come into play. If each of us has a right to our liberty and property, how can another person lay claim to a portion of the life or some of the property of a medical professional in order to fulfill their so-called right to health care? By claiming a "right" to health care, a person is claiming a "right" to a portion of the life and property of another individual. Sure, you could argue that the medical professional will be compensated for his time and property with money. Fine, but where did the money come from? Certainly not from the person exercising his "right" to health care. You don't pay for those things you have a "right" to. The money, in all probability, comes from a taxpayer. So, in the final analysis, it is the taxpayer who is being deprived of a portion of his life and his property in order to fulfill some stranger's "right" to health care.

Sorry, but we need to pause while I dump another quote on you. During Clinton's effort to nationalize our health care, the First Lady, a.k.a The Smartest Woman and the Greatest Lawyer in the World, met with a group of congressmen to discuss her health care plan. One of those congressmen, troubled by the possibility that the government might be choosing people's doctors for them, asked Hillary whether or not individuals would be free to chose their own doctors. Her response? We must stop thinking of the individual and start thinking about what is best for society. So much for individual rights. Let's hear it for the common good.

Once you have established that a person has a right to a portion of another person's life or property, where do you draw the limits? Does the "right" to health care carry forward to a "right" to a home? Does it evolve into a "right" to a pantry full of food, and a closet stocked with the latest fashions?

Just where does all this stop?

This is a question that Liberals don't have to answer so long as they aren't dealing with the concept of individual rights, so long as the rights of the individual are subordinated to the needs of society.

The reality is that under our Constitution no person has a right to anything, other than a trial by jury, that requires any individual to involuntarily surrender a portion of his life or property. This presents quite an obstacle to the Liberal dream of omnipotent government. Ignore the individual, and maybe you can get by with ignoring these rights.

There is another reason why Liberals aren't on friendly terms with the concept of the individual. In a word — responsibility.

How many times have you scratched your head in disbelief, or spoken in harsh terms to your radio or television, when you read or hear society blamed for the actions of some individual.

A child is murdered; a woman is raped; a bomb goes off outside an abortion clinic . . . and we hear our Leftist commentators and politicians place the blame on society.

Well, if you ignore the concept of the individual, if you only think in terms of groups, where else are you going to place the blame? If you hold the individual who committed that crime responsible for his actions, then you will be compelled to hold the individual living in poverty up to the same standards. In this country, with our tremendous opportunities available for all, a person is no less responsible for his or her poverty than he is for his criminal activity.

For the Liberal, once you seek to hold an individual responsible for his actions, you trigger the erosion of your cherished dream for a collective society operating for the greatest good for the greatest number.

DECISIONS, DECISIONS

I have a confession. I just absolutely love tweaking Liberals.

I know just the words, statements, and phrases that will launch them out of their socks and into orbit.

Here's one such statement:

> *Barring extreme physical and mental disabilities, each and every one of us is where we are today — be it poor or wealthy, happy or sad, on the streets or in a condo, in a Mercedes or a rusted-out Pinto — because of the choices we have made during our lives. It's the choices we have made that put us where we are, not the choices others have made for us.*

This statement brings the mental lava boiling to the surface of many people.

First, it bothers Liberals because they don't like the idea that people are in any way responsible for their lots in life. Liberals believe that people are either lucky or unlucky and that it is government that must compensate for the fickle finger of fate.

If you convince people that they, not government, are actually responsible for their fate, the role of government becomes less important. This would make big-government Liberals very unhappy indeed.

The statement also brings howls of pain from life's losers.

Imagine that you are forty years old and still renting an apartment. You have a six-year-old car that isn't paid for, not one penny in a savings account, no retirement plan, you are starting your fourteenth job next Monday, and you are getting a bit weary of seeing your face on the "Deadbeat Dads" public service announcement on television.

Along comes some right-wing reactionary[10] clown saying you are in that position because of the choices you have made during your life.

Like hell! It's not your fault that you can't keep a job. All of those people you were working for were just unreasonable in their demands. You couldn't control the traffic that made you late so many times. And it certainly wasn't your fault that your car kept breaking down. Lousy American cars.

Savings? Retirement? How in the world can you save anything, what with the price of a six-pack and all? Those greedy businessmen just won't pay you enough to allow you to save.

And what about that child support? That judge knew that you couldn't afford to pay that much money in child

---

[10] What the hell does "reactionary" mean, anyway?

support! You have to live, too! Sure, you could have sent her something every month and she might have been satisfied, but she's just trying to ruin your life and you aren't going to fall for that again.

Those people out there with their own homes and their good jobs and fancy cars . . . they were just lucky! They got all the breaks. Nobody out there even wants to give you a chance.

Our whining little friend just can't — or won't — see reality.

Obviously he isn't educated well enough or doesn't have the job skills to get a good, high-paying job. If you could rewind a tape of his life and watch it on fast forward, you would see him making choice after choice that led to his failure to acquire an education. The choice to clown around in class rather than pay attention. The choice to watch television rather than do homework. The choice to play touch football with other kids rather than study for that test. The grand overview will show that he chose not to become educated.

The poor choices kept mounting up. The choice not to leave home earlier so that traffic wouldn't make him late for work. The choice to spend money on a fishing trip instead of keeping his car in running condition. The choice to leave work early for a beer with the guys instead of staying a bit longer to wrap up some loose ends. The choice to turn down that after-hours training program that could have given him more job skills.

And who can imagine the choices he made that got him into his child-support trouble? At the head of the list might be the choice to have children that he and his wife could not yet afford to raise. This led to financial hardships in the marriage (the number one cause of divorce, by the way) and finally to his "Deadbeat Dad" picture on television.

So why does our sad friend get so outraged when I come yammering along with my admonition that his own choices put him where he is?

Simple. It's because he is being told that he is responsible for what has happened to him. Him. Not his boss, not his teachers, not his wife, not the children, not the judge . . . but him.

If you haven't already noticed it, you soon will — people will do anything, say anything, believe anything to escape accepting responsibility for their own lives.

One of the greatest signs of maturity in any individual are the words, "It's my fault. I'm responsible. I made some really stupid decisions. But I'm not going to let it happen again." If you ever hear someone utter those words, hire him. Once you get about ten of them around, you can own the world.

Don't wait until it is too late to recognize the importance of good decision making. Human beings are the only creatures who have the ability to analyze several complicated courses of action and then choose the one that they think will best move them toward their goal. That's your gift. Don't waste it.

If you make the right choices, revel in them. Celebrate your success.

If you make poor choices, accept responsibility for them. Remember, there are always more choices to be made, and the right ones will move you further toward your own idea of success and happiness.

And when those Liberals tell you that you are just a victim of a poor economy, or that you are being oppressed by an unfriendly marketplace, try to remember their motivation. They want to take care of you. They can't do that if you learn to take care of yourself.

THOSE "LESS FORTUNATE"

One of the principal joys of doing a talk show is having the daily opportunity to argue with Liberals. You just can't believe how entertaining it can be to engage in verbal combat with people who are totally void of facts and unable to function at any logical level whatsoever.

The language of the Left becomes impotent in most encounters with a person of moderate verbal skills who can call up reserves of actual facts and present them with a dose of logic. The average Liberal, when caught in such a situation, will most often resort to screams of outrage and shouted charges of insensitivity and hate.

Then he passes out.

There is one phrase from the language of the Left that bothers me more than most, maybe because it is grossly overused and is a particular favorite of Liberals. You have heard it before, and you will continue to hear it, time and time again. It rolls off the tongues of hypersensitive left-wing news anchors and reporters and out of the printers of Liberal newspaper columnists and editorialists with abandon.

The phrase? The "less fortunate."

The phrase is used to refer to people who are not what you might, even in a moment of great charity, call "winners." We're talking about single women with children they can't afford to raise, fathers who abandon their children, high school dropouts with no job prospects, drug addicts and winos begging for money for their next hit, and various other easily recognizable losers.

These people, according to the media, are the "less fortunate."

You read about them in such offerings as, "Welfare reform will make life more difficult for the *less fortunate*," or "The rich can afford to pay a little more in taxes. After all, they have the money, and they should be willing to offer a helping hand to those less fortunate."

When the media types describe the urban outdoorsmen[11], winos, drug addicts, high school dropouts, and various other losers as the "less fortunate," they are implying that those of us who managed to escape this lifestyle and who actually became productive citizens did so because we were simply "more fortunate."

In other words, we were just flat lucky.

---

[11] "Urban outdoorsmen" is a phrase I prefer to use when referring to the so-called "homeless." The phrase gives these pour souls the image of an urban adventurer. You don't take people living in the mountains of Colorado and describe them as "homeless," do you? Those people are outdoorsmen. The only thing that sets them apart from the urban variety is that they have more trees and fewer dumpsters.

Robert Reich, Clinton's former Secretary of Labor and one of his most Liberal advisors, liked to refer to the top 20 percent of income earners in the United States as the "fortunate fifth."

Bring out those dictionaries.

My *Webster's* defines fortunate as "deriving good from an unexpected source."

Think about this for a moment.

Is there anything "unexpected" about deriving good from hard work? Is there anything "unexpected" about deriving good from living a life free of illegal drugs and with only a moderate consumption of alcohol? Is there anything "unexpected" about deriving good from staying in school, not getting pregnant, developing marketable skills, and getting a job?

Hardly.

"Fortune" or "luck" has little to do with it. Luck, they say, is nothing less than opportunity met by preparation.

If you work hard, take advantage of the opportunities you have living in America, and keep your nose clean, then you will succeed, and it won't be because you were fortunate or lucky. It will be because you made smart choices and worked hard.

So, what about the poor? Can we say that their situation in life is unexpected? Are they really the victims of poor fortune?

Hardly.

There is nothing unexpected about failing to find a

good job if you can't read or communicate in the English language.

There is nothing unexpected about not being able to put food on your child's table if you have that child at the age of seventeen or eighteen without any means of supporting him.

There is nothing unexpected about not being able to hold on to a good job if you can't bring your lazy rear end to work each and every day at the proper time, and if you don't have enough character to do what is expected of you, if not more, in return for your paycheck.

There is nothing unexpected about not being able to hold a job, and earn a living, if you make the choice to screw up your mind through the use of illegal drugs or alcohol — and it is a choice, at least initially. Barring mental or physical disaster, poverty is not a matter of luck. It is not a matter of fortune. It is the predictable result of poor decision making, irresponsibility, and laziness.

The poor are not the "less fortunate." They are, instead, the "more irresponsible." They put themselves there, and they drag their children into that status with them. They are the "less prepared," the "less diligent," and the "less able." They weren't unlucky. They did it to themselves.

How, then, do we account for the popularity of the "less fortunate" phrase when referring to people who, more often than not, have done nothing less than completely squander their American birthright?

Here's the logic.

Please observe the workings of the Liberal mind.

Imagine that you are a modern, big-government Liberal. You believe that America is great because of its government, not because of its people. You want more government programs and more spending. You are just brimming over with compassion[12] for the "less fortunate."

You feel their pain.

You are such a good and wonderful person.

One of the things you, as a Liberal, really like about government is that it has the power to use its legal monopoly on the use of force to "level the playing field," so to speak, by redistributing income. You believe wholeheartedly in taking from the rich and giving to the poor. It is not enough to strive for equal opportunity. The true goal must be equality of results. A nice, well-ordered, egalitarian society.

Now, if it is your goal to take money away from people who worked hard and earned it, and then to give that money to people who did not earn it, you are going to need a convincing story, an excuse, a reason.

Well, how's this?

Those people with all the money got that way because they were lucky. They were just fortunate. It's not that they are any smarter or better than anyone else, or that they worked any harder. They were just fortunate. They were in the right place at the right time. They had the

---

[12] As we all know, it is so easy to show compassion with someone else's money.

right skin color. They were lucky because they got to go to a better school.

And what about those people living on the streets or in the homeless shelters, or wasting away in a public housing project with babies they can't afford to raise? Well, those people aren't there because they are less intelligent, or because they didn't work as hard as the others. They just weren't lucky enough. They weren't fortunate enough. They didn't get the breaks everyone else gets. They are the "less fortunate."

So, now that you have convinced yourself (and others) that those people with money were just lucky, and those people without enough money were not as lucky, you find it easier to make a case for just taking money away from those lucky, fortunate folks and giving it to those poor, unlucky, "less fortunate" folks.

After all, it's not like they actually went out there and worked for that money! They didn't sacrifice anything. They were just lucky. They were the "fortunate." All you're doing is just evening out the odds a bit. Gee, that would only be fair, wouldn't it?

One of my favorite big-government Liberals, Missouri democrat Richard Gephardt, reached all-time absurd levels in 1996 in playing up this "fortunate/less fortunate" idea that Liberals love so. He referred to those people in our society who enjoy high incomes as a result of hard work and good decision making as "those who won life's lottery."

Life's lottery? Gephardt thinks we won some lottery?

You stay in school, keep your nose clean, work hard, and make responsible choices, and, as a result, become successful, and Gephardt thinks that you have won a lottery?

What a colossal insult!

Try this. Walk up to someone who has been working sixty-hour weeks since the day he got out of school to become successful and suggest that his comfortable lifestyle is due to nothing more than the right-numbered ping-pong balls falling into the chute.

Then duck.

The motive behind Gephardt's insulting "won life's lottery" remark is the same as for those who use the "less fortunate" phrase. If a person has all of that money because of luck or a lottery drawing, what's the big problem with making him share it? After all, it's not as if he actually worked for it.

Learn this now: Life is not a lottery.

Nobody knows where the ping-pong balls will fall. Nobody knows when luck will strike. But every rational person knows the result of hard work and wise choices. The result is, in a word, success. Success brought on by hard work, not by luck.

AN ENDNOTE:

Several years ago, when there was still a Soviet Union, an Atlanta television station tried an innovative experiment. They traded television reporters with a station in Moscow.

As I had made several trips to Moscow by that time, I

became acquainted with the Russian reporter. He came to America with the typical Leftist baggage. He came fully expecting to see the masses living under the oppression of the wealthy capitalists.

He soon saw the light.

He taught me, and others, that sometimes the best way to see yourself, and your country, is through the eyes of someone from a completely different, in this case Communist, culture.

One day this reporter was sent to one of our welfare housing projects to do a report on his perspective of our "less fortunate" citizens.

After spending a few days researching these welfare recipients and their surroundings, he was ready to film his report.

He stood at the entrance to the welfare housing project and delivered the following line:

"*I came here expecting to find poverty. This isn't poverty, this is laziness.*"

My Russian friend saw through this "less fortunate" nonsense in a real hurry.

That line, however, never made it to the air.

LIBERALS DON'T WANT YOU TO READ THESE BOOKS!

You may have noticed by now that this book is quite small. The reason is simple. It doesn't take many words, and it certainly doesn't take a great deal of brain power, to disclose the basic, hideous truth about Liberals.

I'm a talker, not a writer. One hundred fifty pages or so is about as long as it gets for me.

If you have enjoyed irritating and infuriating your Leftist friends and relatives with some of the ideas presented in this book, perhaps you will want to load up with some heavier weapons. Maybe you would like to delve just a little deeper into the dark world of logic and fact.

For those of you who would like to make a life's work — perhaps even a sport — of bludgeoning Liberals with the club of reality, I have listed here several books which will give you all of the ammunition you need.

A word of warning is needed here. If you are a closet Liberal who has picked up this book by accident, leave the books I have listed here alone! These books could cause some rather severe intellectual discomfort, especially if you are suffering from a desire to single-handedly save humanity from itself, or if you have been diagnosed with Obsessive-Compulsive Compassion Disorder.

Liberals, beware! Avoid these books like the plague.[13]

ATLAS SHRUGGED

This book, written by some Russian immigrant named Ayn Rand, is the big kahuna. Thankfully it is over one thousand pages long, which makes it unattractive to most Liberals who prefer fewer words, larger type, and more pictures.

You may be familiar with the classical image of Atlas struggling to balance Earth on his shoulders. He is stooped over, his legs are bent, and the strain is obvious on his face. Luckily, Atlas is strong, and it appears that he can hold on for quite a while.

What do you suppose might happen, though, if the weight of the globe on Atlas's shoulders kept increasing, getting heavier and heavier until it was almost unbearable? Not only is the increased weight of the world almost unbearable, but Atlas is just not getting his propers for the burden he is shouldering. He is suffering insults and hatred from the very people he is holding up.

Finally, the burden gets to be a bit too much. One final straw, and Atlas shrugs.

This book contains a particularly dangerous speech (at least to our liberal friends) from some character named John Galt. Galt is rather wordy. It took him about four

---

[13] It is also a good idea to avoid clichés like the plague.

hours to deliver this message. You might be able to read it in less time if you don't move your lips.

One bad point: The heroine smokes.

CAMP OF THE SAINTS

This book was written by a Frenchman named Jean Raspail. This is unfortunate, because the book is so good, and people aren't especially eager to read books written by Frenchmen. Another problem is that the book seems to be out of print.

This means that it is really available only in libraries. If Liberals knew what this book contained they would have personal agents in libraries all over the country keeping this book constantly checked out so that it wouldn't damage the mental health of their Leftist friends.

You've heard all of the arguments about immigration reform. Some people actually think that there is something a wee bit wrong about letting people come into this country and then telling the taxpayers that they must provide these newcomers with medical care, a place to live, food, and a nifty little cash income. Liberals call these people greedy and insensitive.

Well, *Camp of the Saints* is a pure wet dream for Liberals who think we ought to change the Immigration and Naturalization Service into an International Welcome Wagon.

Imagine this: Every diseased, uneducated, unemployable, unsocialized, needy, and pathetic person, along with their countless children (each carrying a chicken), from every third-world country on Earth suddenly joins some sort of a mass exodus to the industrialized West.

Literally hundreds of millions of these impoverished people, along with their self-righteous leaders, manage to commandeer every boat that can still float in every obscure harbor in the world, and they all set sail for the coasts of America and Europe. The bodies of the dead are thrown over the sides as this armada makes its way. Their announced intention is to land on the shores of the wealthy countries of the world and demand their "right" to a share of the wealth. To be fed, clothed, sheltered, and cared for.

The great joy of this book is watching the professional do-gooders do battle with one another. They know disaster is on the way, but their grand sense of social responsibility and their obsessive-compulsive Liberal ethic just won't let them say no. Those with the gift of logical thought will love the depiction of the mental burnout as the Liberals of the world shout "My God! These people are coming to *my* door and they want *my* house and *my* money!"

It gets rich when tens of thousands of these rusted-out ships suddenly start anchoring a hundred yards or so off the coasts of Europe and the United States. I get a particular thrill when thousands of them anchor off the shores of France.

Not a pretty sight. And not a comfortable read for those still steeped in left-wing emotionalism.

If you do happen to see this book sitting on a library shelf, check it out for a Liberal friend . . . one whom you want to get rid of.

THE LAW

The Law is now around 150 or so years old. To be exact, it was published as a pamphlet in June of 1850. Strangely enough, it's another book by a Frenchman, Frederic Bastiat. It is amazing that such wonderful (but dangerous) books can be written in such an incomprehensible, whiny language.

This is the book that turned me.

Yes, dear reader, remember that I, too, was once a dream-filled, holier-than-thou, super-compassionate Liberal. At Texas A&M, I was in bed with Students for a Democratic Society. I spent countless hours moaning and grieving for the exploited, the oppressed, and the less fortunate.

Then I read *The Law.*

Bastiat wrote the book around the time of the French Revolution.[14] There were some powerful people back then who were urging a socialist government and economy for France. Bastiat, an economist, thought that this wasn't such a great idea.

Bastiat wrote *The Law* in an effort to explain why socialism would be a disaster for France . . . and why it simply would not work.

This book explains, better than any writing or any person ever has, before or since, just what the true purpose and function of government and the law is.

The Law is very short. Much shorter than this mess. It

---

[14] French revolutions are not surprising to those of us who find the French revolting.

is short because it doesn't really take too many words to explain the role of the law in a free society. It takes many more words to explain the role of the law and government in a society that is not so free.[15]

OK. So now we have three books on this list. One by a Russian and two by Frenchmen. We need to get at least one American author on this list. So, after an extensive search, I found a book by an American author that will, if read by a doctrinaire Liberal, cause severe mental anguish, not to mention an emotional overload.

THE WAY THINGS OUGHT TO BE

This book is by Rush Limbaugh. Perhaps you've heard of him. He is our token American here. *All* talk show hosts owe Rush Limbaugh a debt of gratitude, whether they agree with him or not.

Rush Limbaugh has done for talk radio what Arnold Palmer did for golf. Before Arnie came along, many professional golfers had to give lessons to make ends meet. After Palmer, professional golfers needed weight training just to carry their wallets around.

Limbaugh's two books are good, really! He shows excellent insight into just how we got ourselves into this mess . . . and how we will get ourselves out.

---

[15] Have you read a copy of the Federal Register lately?

QUICK POINTS!

One of the most powerful human emotions is envy. It is also one of the most easily manipulated emotions.

Politicians learned hundreds of years ago that people who had little material wealth were incredibly jealous of those who had more than they did. This deep-seated envy was ripe for exploitation — and the exploitation has been running rampant for generations.

There are far more voters in this country who do not consider themselves to be rich than there are voters who would claim that title. This means that politicians can slam the rich, damn the rich, tax the rich, roast the rich, and eat the rich without putting too many votes in jeopardy.

Note, please, the ways that Liberals love to refer to the rich. We have "filthy rich," "ungodly rich," "robber barons," and many other titles that are somewhat less than complimentary.

This anti-wealth propaganda has had an effect. When you poll Americans about the wealthy, you will find that the majority of people feel that rich people came about their money in some dishonest manner. They had crooked lawyers. They cheated on their income taxes. They exploited others. They consumed more than their "fair share" of the world's resources, and so on.

There is a deep-seated psychological need for those who are not wealthy to assume that the wealthy got that way through evil and illegal means.

If you recognize that most wealthy people got that way through hard work, the wise use of their power of choice, and the willingness to take risks, you are stuck with the problem of figuring out just why you're not up there with them. What's the matter? Don't you want to work hard? Are you afraid to take risks? Are you not willing to put time and thought into your decision-making process?

Naw . . . this isn't going to work. If you agree that the rich are good, then you have to develop excuses about why you're not wallowing in money.

But . . . if you adopt the attitude that the rich are evil — that they used crooked lawyers to take advantage of innocent people, that they exploited their workers and ravaged the environment — you will find it easier to make excuses for your own lack of success.

After all, you aren't evil. You don't have a crooked lawyer. You don't exploit innocent workers or take advantage of innocent waifs, and you aren't an enemy of the environment.

That's why you aren't rich. It's because you are good. And those rich people are bad.

Wow! What a wonderful rationalization! It sure gets you off the hook, doesn't it? And it makes you a willing myrmidon to any politician who wants to exploit this mindset for his own personal gain.

SOUNDS SORT OF FAMILIAR

I have never been one to find Communists under every bed. Frankly, religious zealots have been more worrisome to me than Communists, even before the fall of the Soviet Union and the Berlin Wall. At least the Communists never tried to tell us that God gave them express permission to rule.

There has been one little phrase that, over the years, has been closely associated with communism and socialism. It appears in the *Communist Manifesto*. You've heard it before; now here it is in writing: **"From each according to his ability. To each according to his needs."**

I have noticed a return of this little ditty during recent years. It seems to be on the minds of a lot of Liberals in the Clinton administration.

As soon as Clinton took office in 1993, he started pushing his retroactive tax increase on upper-income Americans. "The rich," he said, "need to pay their fair share." When people asked him why he planned to raise taxes only on the wealthy and not across the board, he replied that he wanted to hit the rich with a tax increase "because that's where the money is."

"From each according to his ability."

After the voter revolution of 1994, the Republicans took a majority position in Congress. They immediately started talking about tax cuts. As luck would have it, many of these tax cuts would benefit the rich. What a concept! Giving a tax break to the very group that pays the huge bulk of the taxes!

The Clinton administration wasted no time at all in decrying the idea of allowing the rich to keep any more of the money they earn. Clinton's Labor Secretary, Robert Reich, said that such a tax cut was not warranted because, after all, the rich "don't need the money."

"To each according to his needs."
It all somehow sounds so familiar . . . but I'm probably just imagining things.

THE TRUTH ABOUT GUN CONTROL
We certainly aren't going to solve the gun control mess here, but there are a few things you need to think about as the debate rages on:

1. Those who favor gun control never seem to have any plan to take guns out of the hands of criminals. All the plans for gun registration, waiting periods, concealed-weapons laws, and ownership bans affect only those people who obey the law. These aren't the people who are using guns to rob, rape, and murder.

More than 90 percent of the guns used in crimes are obtained outside of regular commerce. This means that they aren't bought at gun stores, and they aren't registered to the person who used them in the crime. This means that laws aimed at retail gun sales don't even begin to address the problem.

2. Guns don't kill people. People kill people with guns. I am both amused and outraged when I read headlines like "Gun Kills Three" or "Guns Responsible for Deaths." So far as I know, there has never been one single case where a gun has, on its own, decided that it would be a nifty idea to hop out of that nightstand drawer it has been trapped in and head on down to the local convenience store for a quick robbery.

The gun control crowd likes to blame violence on the guns. That way they aren't actually breaking one of the most basic Liberal rules: "You shall not hold an individual responsible for his actions."

3. In any given year about 99.98 percent of all of the privately owned handguns in the entire country are not used in a murder. About 99.6 percent of the privately owned handguns are not used in a crime of any description. Wow! This really shows the urgency for strong gun control, doesn't it?

Here's an idea: Why not concentrate on the small minority of people who are using guns for criminal purposes, rather than the vast majority who own their guns peacefully and at no risk to anyone who doesn't mean them harm?

WHY DO THESE BEDWETTERS
KEEP WINNING ELECTIONS?

Good question. The majority of the people in this country would call themselves either Centrist or Conservative. So why do Leftists continue to walk off with so many of the political prizes?

I think the answer lies in the basic mental makeup of those who call themselves Liberals and those who consider themselves Conservative.

Remember, Liberals think and act in terms of groups. They are collectivists. They live, eat, sleep, and think in terms of their group identity.

Because of their identification with the group, and their need to be a part of the group, it is much easier to organize them into group action, such as voting.

Conservatives, on the other hand, eschew their group identity for their individual reality. They aren't easily organized, and they cannot be prompted into collective action as easily as Liberals. If they vote, it is the result of an individual decision, not part of a group movement.

Believe me, Liberals know this, and they like it that way.

YOUR INCOME TAX WITHHOLDING

Someday you may wonder why your income taxes are taken out of your paycheck *before* you ever even see the money. Why can't you just write a check for your income taxes the same way you do for your car payment and child support?

Because the government doesn't want a tax revolt,

that's why.

You may be surprised to know that, up until World War II, that is exactly what American wage earners did. They took their entire paycheck home and wrote a check to the government every year for the taxes they owed.

During World War II, the Political Class told us that they needed to speed up the cash flow a bit in order to pay for the war effort. No problem, the American people were in a mood to do anything it took. So the government started withholding taxes from paychecks before the wage earners ever saw them.

Here's the kicker: We were promised that as soon as the war ended the withholding would end, and we would go back to the old way of paying those taxes once a year.

In case you haven't noticed, the war is over. It's been over for quite some time now.

So, why is withholding still with us?

Very simple. In spite of the promises that were made, withholding is still with us because politicians know with absolute certainty that there would be an instantaneous and universal tax revolt if people actually had to pay their taxes by check.

Our Political Class could not continue the wild spending spree that keeps it in power if the Taxpayer Class had any idea at all just how much it is paying in taxes.

Oh, do you think that most people know anyway? It's right there on their check stub, right?

Fair enough. You go ahead and believe that . . . right up

until next April 15 rolls around. Then give this little experiment a try:

Walk up to a couple of people in your office, or some friends, and ask them how much tax they had to pay this year. Remember, do this right around April 15 so that the vision of that tax return will still be sharp in their minds.

Ten to one you get this mindless response: "Oh, I didn't have to pay any! I'm getting some back!"

Of all the brain-dead, moronic things you will ever hear a human being say, this one takes the cake. This person doesn't even know how much he paid in taxes. He thinks the government is "giving" him something back!

Don't you know politicians just love this?

Carry it a bit further. Ask some of your friends what they make. Damned if some of them won't say, "I take home about $_____ a week."

"Take home? I didn't ask you how much you took home. I asked you how much you made!"

Our leaders have us thinking in terms of "take-home pay." We have been so blinded by this withholding nonsense that we don't even know how much money we are making anymore. We just know how much the Imperial Federal Government left for us to spend on ourselves.

THE MINIMUM WAGE

I just thought I would mention this one here, because it really frosts me big time!

I am sick to death of hearing Liberals talk about how

difficult it is to raise a family on the minimum wage.

Why oh why doesn't someone walk up to one of these people and say, "Hey, pal, you're not supposed to raise a family on minimum wage. If you don't have the job skills or the wherewithal to earn more than the minimum wage, then you don't have any business having children, because you can't afford to raise them!"

One of the greatest social crimes a couple can commit is to have a baby that they cannot afford to raise.

THE RICH GET RICHER, AND THE POOR GET POORER

This one is so easy to explain. The rich keep getting richer because they keep doing the things that made them rich. Ditto for the poor. See how simple all this is?

HATE SPEECH AND HATE CRIMES

As you now know, our friends on the Left don't become particularly elated at the idea of dealing with the thoughts and ideas of another person on a factual and logical level. A poke in the eye with a nice sharp stick would suit them better.

Liberals have developed time-proven tactics to delay these nasty and uncomfortable encounters with Conservative or Libertarian ideas. One of their most successful ploys is to attempt to demonize those thoughts and ideas, to discredit them, and render them unworthy of use in public discourse.

The best way to accomplish this is to tie those thoughts and ideas to a strong negative image.

Everybody will probably agree that hate is a negative emotion. People don't particularly like people who hate, people don't want to be hated, and people will seek to avoid being seen in the company of hateful people.

Listen to Liberals who are under fire from the Right. Instead of responding in a logical and rational manner to the criticisms, they start a cacophony of shrill screams about "hate speech."

It is easy to see why they chose to hide behind this "hate speech" nonsense. It's so mindlessly easy and convenient. Someone criticizes you or a program you support. You find yourself faced with the task of responding to the criticism. You realize, though, that responding might require an exercise in logic — something Liberals are particularly bad at. So, if valid points are brought up — points that you don't particularly want to deal with — you can just brand the comments as hate speech and proudly proclaim your determination not to respond. How noble and wonderfully sensitive it sounds. What a wonderful, sensitive, and caring person you are when you say, "I won't dignify that hate speech with a response."

Bill Clinton knows the routine. He has used this "hate speech" phrase quite a bit, particularly in reference to people who are critical of his presidency.

That brings us to talk radio, a subject I know just a little about.

Talk radio is an element of the media that is not permeated with left-wing extremists suffering from Obsessive-Compulsive Compassion Disorder. This is not mere happenstance. There is a good, logical reason behind the dominance of talk radio by Libertarians and Conservatives. Why?

We'll take a little detour here and explain:

A talk show host will spend around fifteen hours a week talking to, responding to, and arguing with a variety of callers. If you spend fifteen hours a week in conversation with people, and if you can't deal logically and truthfully with the issues that become a part of your show, you will never survive as a talk show host. You will soon be exposed as a simple-minded phony. You will be left taking about your feelings while the callers bury you with facts and logic. Simply stated, this spells doom for most Liberals who give talk radio a shot. Road Kill. The only way a Liberal can survive as a radio talk show host is to counter their lack of logical debate skills with an extremely enter- taining personality. How many Liberals do you know with an entertaining personality? Without one or the other they soon get devoured by sharp callers and are found by their program director cowering and sobbing in the fetal posi- tion in a dark corner of the studio. It's not a pretty sight.

All of this means that talk radio is not particularly pop- ular with Leftists. You won't be surprised to learn that Clinton is particularly upset with talk radio. This is a fact that gives me enormous pride and satisfaction.

Clinton as much as blamed talk radio for the failure of the grand government takeover of health care engineered by his lovely wife, The Smartest Woman In the World. Fact is, he was right. Talk radio was really the only element of the media that really delved into the nuts and bolts of Clinton's socialized medicine plan and presented those loose nuts to the American people. It spelled the end of his pet program. Clinton wasn't what you would call "grateful." This is when talk show hosts really started feeling the heat.

Clinton was presented with a golden opportunity to turn the thumb screws on talk radio after the hideous bombing of the federal office building in Oklahoma City. He practically blamed the carnage on the preachers of hate that take to the nation's airwaves and dare to criticize his policies. How dare these damnable people express anything other than praise for the American government and his administration?

The Left immediately picked up on Clinton's lead. Here they had a chance to not only step up their attack on talk radio, but they also had the bonus opportunity of tying their radio nemesis to a grotesque terrorist act.

Talk radio has taken much of the heat for keeping the pressure on Clinton for the innumerable scandals that have thus far permeated his presidency. Thank you, you say? Don't mention it. We were proud to do it.

This constant bombardment of the American people with torrents of facts and logic about the various blemishes on the Clintonista regime finally got on the Liberal's last good nerve. They retaliated. Now they have bestowed on talk radio a nifty new name! The new politically correct word for talk radio is . . . Hate Radio!

Sad to say, this Liberal ploy has worked. We have arrived at the point where any Conservative principle or statement is simply dismissed, by both the Liberals and their dog washers in the media, as being hate speech. If it's on radio, it's hate radio. Once you've called it hate, you no longer have to deal with it. It is all too simple.

If there's anything that Liberals hate more than having to deal with logic and facts, it's suffering criticism. I don't blame them. If I were them, I'd feel picked on, too. Let's face it, the overpowering truth here is that Liberals are absurdly easy to criticize. Their demeanor just begs for it. It's like shooting ducks in a barrel.

The Liberal solution to unwanted criticism is to use the same tactics that work so well for avoiding facts and logic: neutralize legitimate criticism by tying it to a negative image.

How about "bashing" as an image?

That should do it. That's negative enough.

We'll call it "Liberal bashing," or "Clinton bashing," or "Hillary bashing."

So, in the eyes of the Liberal, you aren't criticizing someone; you're "bashing" them. There exists no possibility for any legitimate criticism of a Liberal or a Liberal thought or ideal. It's all "bashing."

Only Liberals can be bashed. You don't believe me? Ask any card-carrying Liberal! If it's the Liberal who's doing the criticizing, with a Conservative taking the blows, it's not bashing. To the Liberal, it's merely telling the truth. Note, please, that you have never heard the phrase "Conservative bashing," "Starr bashing," or "Gingrich bashing" in our Liberal-dominated media.

Remember, Liberals believe that the truth is known only to Liberals . . . and it's subject to change.

So, now we have the Liberal concept of "hate speech" and its cousin, "bashing." Liberals successfully took the expression of thoughts and ideas that run contrary to their whiny, hyper-compassionate philosophy and labeled these thoughts and ideas as "hate."

Having accomplished this, the next step for the Left was to take these demonized thoughts and ideas and try to actually criminalize them. Make them illegal.

How do you criminalize thoughts and ideas in a country that is supposed to guarantee free speech? No problem. The liberal elite merely developed the concept of "hate crimes"!

You've heard the "hate crime" phrase bandied about in the media for some time now. Various local governments are tripping over themselves trying to get the proper hate crimes legislation passed.

So what, exactly, is a hate crime? The phrase just begs for a definition. Let's give it a shot. It's not easy.

Murder, you can define. Ditto for rape and armed robbery. But just how, pray tell, do you define a hate crime? How does a hate crime differ from an ordinary, run-of-the-mill, everyday crime?

If a person is killed in a hate crime, is he more or less dead than someone simply killed for his money or car, because he was driving too slow in the fast lane, or because he was simply in the wrong place at the wrong time?

Will the wife and children of a man killed in a carjacking take comfort in the fact that at least it wasn't a hate crime? *"It was a terrible, senseless crime. But we are so comforted by the knowledge that the person who murdered George didn't hate him."* Yeah, right. Works for me.

Is the person who kills out of hate or prejudice any more

dangerous to our society than a simple predator who kills for drugs or because he wants someone else's property?

Dead is dead. Murder is murder. Robbery is robbery. Rape is rape. Period. It doesn't matter how the predator felt about you. You're dead, robbed, or raped.

Liberals (not surprisingly) don't particularly like to spend time defining terms. I, however, suffer from no such aversion.

A hate crime is a run-of-the-mill, regular crime despoiled by the politically incorrect thoughts of the perpetrator.

There is only one thing that differentiates a regular murder from a hate-crime murder. That one element is the state of mind of the person who committed the crime — in other words, the thought processes of the person who pulled the trigger. The difference is one of motive. Nothing else.

Motive, as I'm sure you realize, is a thought process. This means that it is the element of thought that changes our ordinary crime into a horrible, antisocial, politically incorrect hate crime.

A hate crime, then, is a thought crime. With this hate-crime concept, the Left has managed to accomplish its goal of making an individual criminally liable not only for the actual criminal act that he committed, but also for the thoughts he harbored when committing the crime.

In the minds of the proponents of hate-crime legislation, a random act of violence against an individual takes on increased seriousness if certain thought processes are involved. If the thought processes are not politically acceptable, the act becomes a hate crime. We have a thought crime piggybacking on a crime against a person or property. A person is being punished, or is having his punishment increased, depending on what he was thinking.

Thoughts as crimes. A Liberal nirvana. The criminal codification of political correctness.

On November 19, 1997, Bill Clinton issued a statement saying that we needed to expand federal authority in the area of hate crimes, particularly in relationship to hate crimes against gays and handicapped people.

So, once again, the man who told us that "the era of big government is over" called for yet more federal involvement in our lives . . . and, in this case, in our very thought processes.

Another big problem with hate-crime laws is that they create different classes of victims. If someone attacks me because they want my car, and I'm murdered, the punishment may be less and the category of crime would be different than if someone attacks a gay man and murders him because he doesn't like gay men. In both cases, murder committed — man dead. But my murder is somehow less egregious than the murder of the homosexual. Pardon me, and I hope you'll excuse me for this insensitivity, but I just don't happen to see it that way.

In a society where equal protection under the law is supposed to be the noble standard, there is no room to create different classes of victims. Hate-crime legislation places a different, government-assigned value on the life, liberty, and property rights of people based on their color, religion, sexual orientation, national origin, physical ability, or whatever.

Clinton (sorry . . . just can't bring myself to put the words "President" and "Clinton" together — gag reflex, you know) says, "All Americans deserve protection from hate."

Say what? Have we suddenly acquired another right here? Do we now have the right to be protected from hate? Fantastic! Let's just add this to the right to a job, the right to a living wage, the right to a condo, the right to breast implants, and the right to a satisfying sex life.

It is so nice to know that I now have the right not to be hated, and that Bill Clinton is ready to bring the full force of the Imperial Federal Government of the United States to bear on anyone who dares to dislike me. After all, I "deserve" it. The next time someone says he hates me, what should I do? Should I swear out a warrant? Is it a federal crime, or just a local ordinance? Do I call the FBI? Will Janet Reno appoint a special prosecutor? Just how will the person be punished? Can I sue him? What if someone just says he hates my show? What if they hate this book? Do I deserve to be protected from that?

Let's try to get just a bit serious here. Hating me is not a violation of my rights. I have no right to be loved. I have no right to be liked. I have no right not to be hated. It is not the role of the federal government to keep me from being hated . . . or to protect me from hate.

It is the role of government to seek to apprehend and prosecute those who deprive me of life, liberty, or property, whether it's out of hate or just a desire for my stuff. The offender should be prosecuted for the crime he has committed. (Followed by, in all probability, a slap on the wrist and a few minutes of community service.) What they happen to think about me is absolutely beside the point.

With the big push in Washington to deal with "hate crimes" and Clinton's pronouncement that all Americans deserve to be protected from hate, how long is it before dissent to the Washington status quo will, in and of itself, become a crime?

I hope you just absolutely loved this chapter. If you didn't, I'm swearing out a warrant tomorrow.

48
SECONDS

This chapter has absolutely nothing to do with politics, Liberals, Libertarians, Socialists, Conservatives, or Libertines.

You bought this book. You're reading it, and here's a little thought I wanted to pass along before you move on to something else.

Imagine that you're flying a small, single-engine airplane on a nice VFR day. "VFR" stands for "Visual Flight Rules," which means you're not flying in or near clouds and you can see where you're going. You can look for other airplanes, and they can look for you, thus hopefully avoiding a chance, unhappy, mid-air encounter. It's a typical hot and hazy summer day, but you can still see the ground and the horizon. You have a good feel for the "attitude" of the airplane: whether it is turning left or right, descending or climbing. With this type of visibility, you aren't going to inadvertently fly into the ground or a cloud full of rocks. The engine is purring, and all is well with the world.

Suddenly you notice you can't see the horizon anymore. The haze has become a bit thicker. A few seconds later you can't see the ground. All of the references you were depending on outside the windows of that airplane are suddenly gone! Even the tips of your wings seem to fade away into the haze!

You have flown into the clouds.

This is not good.

This is what pilots call IMC, or "Instrument Meteorological Conditions." You, my friend, are flying on instruments.

If you are a trained instrument pilot, no problem. If you're not, the statistics say you have forty-eight seconds to live. Maybe fifty.

Up until this point in your flight you have been depending, in large part, on your visual references. You could look at the horizon and tell if your wings were level, not to mention which side of your airplane is up and which side is down. You could look at the ground, or directly ahead, to see if you were turning or flying straight. You might have glanced at your instrument panel every few seconds to see if you were holding your altitude, but, by and large, your eyes were outside of the airplane.

When you flew into the clouds, though, it became a different matter. Without those familiar visual references, it's only you and those dials and gauges on your instrument panel.

Suddenly your senses tell you that the airplane is turning! You can feel the movement — the left wing dips and you feel strange pressures against your seat. You take a quick look at the instrument panel but quickly discount what those instruments tell you. Your body and senses tell you one thing. Those gauges tell you another. You decide to trust your own senses. After all, they haven't failed you yet! You have been in the clouds for about fifteen seconds now. You have about thirty-three seconds left.

You're still fighting the definite feeling that the airplane is turning. You turn the yoke just a bit to the left. There! That feels better!

Twenty-seven seconds.

You take another look at the instruments. Funny, they show you with your left wing down. That compass is turning, and the altimeter is moving. Now you're convinced that something must be wrong with those instruments. You're going to trust the messages from your body, not the instruments. You twist the yoke just a bit more . . . there! That feels about right.

Twenty seconds.

Many miles away, some air traffic controller is watching you on his radar screen. He can see that you are turning sharply to the left and losing altitude! He can't get you on the radio, though. You're too busy trying to fly the airplane, and, besides, you aren't on his radio frequency.

Fifteen seconds.

You think you have everything under control. You should fly out of this cloud any moment now. As soon as you get on the ground you're going to sign up for those instrument flying lessons. You're not going to get caught like this again!

Ten seconds.

Suddenly you fly out of the cloud — right out of the bottom of the cloud.

Eight seconds.

Something's wrong! You're in a steep bank to the left and losing altitude quickly! The ground is spinning in your windshield!

Five seconds.

You yank back on the yoke! You have to stop this descent! The airplane shudders, and the left wing drops some more!

Three seconds.

The airplane stalls and spins into the ground.

Zero seconds.

Time's up, and you've just been given the celestial pink slip. In a few hours the inspectors from the National Transportation Safety Board are going to be picking over the wreckage of your aircraft trying to figure out just how and why you died.

The answer always seems to be the same. Incapable of interpreting and trusting the instruments, the untrained pilot will instead rely on his own senses or intuition . . . and eventually come spinning out of the bottom of the cloud to his death.

A pilot in that situation needs to put his full faith in something completely outside his own senses. That's where those instruments on the panel of his airplane come into play. They tell him where he is. What his airplane is doing.

And just what he needs to do to stay alive and find his way back to clear skies. The pilot's body and "feelings" are going to tell him that those instruments are wrong. Actually, it's stronger than that. The pilot's body is going to insist that those instruments are wrong.

If he believes and trusts in his body and senses, he dies. If puts his faith in those instruments, he survives.

Your journey through life is much like that pilot's trip.

We, like many pilots, are fortunate that we spend most of our personal lives flying VFR. Our visibility is reasonably clear. We can see our goals, as well as the obstacles that stand in our way. We usually know in what direction we are heading, and we can tell whether or not we are making good speed. We can see the horizon, and that helps us keep our "wings" level. All is well in our little corner of the world.

Then, sooner or later, we fly into a cloud.

The truth is that it is extremely unlikely you are going to complete life's journey without encountering some IMC. Sooner or later we all fly into rough weather. For some of us the trip is short. Others have a long way to go before they can see the horizon again.

When you hit the "soup" (and eventually you will), if you try to rely on your senses, on your "feel," on your intellect and intuition to get you back into the clear weather, you stand a good chance of becoming another forty-eight-second statistic.

Just as with that pilot who flew into the clouds, we need instruments that we can refer to and put our absolute faith in when we go from the sunshine to the rain. We need instruments that will give us unerring guidance back into the clear weather where we can once again rely on our vision and our senses to continue our journey.

I'm talking about faith.

If the pilot in the clouds puts his faith in those instruments, he will live to see the numbers at the end of that runway. If he relies just on his own feelings and hunches, he is going to end up digging his own grave with his propeller. If you find something to put your faith in during times of trouble and stress, during the times you are in the clouds, you will survive to see happier times.

It is not my intent to preach religion here. There are other writers who are much better at that than I. I am merely suggesting that a core belief in something that surpasses your intellect, your "feel," or your "senses" will serve you well in troubling times.

Occasionally we really do get too smart for our own good. We enter these dangerous times when we feel that we "know it all."

But nobody can ever know it all.

You are going to need some instruments to turn to when you can't see the ground.

For some, those instruments can be found in the Bible. For others, it might be the Koran or the Torah. You probably already have a sense of where your own set of instruments lies, but your sense of intellectual dominance may have dulled your faith.

Right now you might think that your body and mind are better guides out of the darkness. Follow that hunch and start counting your forty-eight seconds.

Have faith in your instruments. Practice flying on those instruments until it becomes second nature to you. Practice until you can make that transition from sunshine to clouds and back again with ease.

Practice and keep practicing. Believe and keep believing. When all of your senses tell you that the instruments are wrong, have faith — and happy landings!

BUYING A DEFEAT-PROOF LIBERAL CONGRESS

"A democracy cannot exist as a permanent form of government. It can only exist until the voters discover that they can vote themselves money from the public treasury."
— Alexander Tyler

"In general the art of government consists in taking as much money as possible from one class of citizens to give to the other."
— Voltaire

"In the end they will lay their freedom at our feet and say to us, 'Make us your slaves, but feed us."
— Dosteovsky's *Grand Inquisitor*

Wow! How about that? Starting a chapter with actual quotes! It's enough to make you think I'm a real author!

This is a new chapter of *The Terrible Truth About Liberals* for the paperback edition. Some of the themes explored in a preceding chapter "Who Really Pays the Taxes?" are updated and expanded here. I readdress this because it is now painfully clear that the left is attempting, with great success, to use our tax structure to build a defeat-proof liberal congress.

Most of the themes of this book have been developed, nurtured during the course of my 30+ years in talk radio. The difference between presenting and arguing these ideas on radio and in a book is that the call-in radio listeners can use their telephones to fight back. Their challenges have helped me fine-tune my opinions. As I've written elsewhere (I think), this doesn't happen to anchors, commentators, columnists, and editorial writers.

After a particularly rousing diatribe from The Talkmaster (that would be me), some listeners will call with some version of a call-to-arms for another revolution. My response has always been essentially the same: "You have a chance for a revolution every two years. The ballot box. Try it. It works!"

I would tell my listeners that every two years they have the opportunity to completely change 100 percent of the membership of the House of Representatives and one-third of the U.S. Senate. A peaceful, lawful, bloodless revolution. All they have to do is remember their anger, remember their concerns, and take a few moments out of their busy days on the first Tuesday in November and go vote!

Just what is it about people who will camp out in front of a ticket window for 24 hours to purchase tickets for the latest rap or rock group, but who can't find 45 minutes to participate in deciding who will have the power to plunder their bank accounts, limit their economic and social freedom, and put their very lives in jeopardy? Is there any way we could make voting more like a rock concert, a wrestling match, or a bingo game? Maybe that would rustle up some of the dead wood.

Then again, maybe it's too late. If it's not too late, there sure isn't much time left.

My mind is starting to change. The realization is dawning that the ballot box is very close to becoming worthless. Worthless, that is, to the people in this country who actually want to see a return to limited government, lower taxes, and more personal responsibility.

Over a period of decades the left (and we're principally talking Democrats here) has been changing the use and purpose of the ballot box. Where it once was the tool of a knowledgeable and concerned citizen, it is now becoming an instrument of plunder for America's non- and under-achievers.

For the past eight years I have been digesting a particularly distressing compilation of statistics from the IRS. These are the statistics on just who is paying what taxes. As I said, we covered this earlier in the book. Now, here's your update:

Every year the picture becomes more depressing. Every single year the burden for federal income taxes gets shifted more and more to the top-income earners while more and more of those in the lower- and middle-income levels are relieved of any income tax burden at all. Extrapolating the latest figures from 1998, and the projections for following years, by 2001 approximately 39 percent of all federal income taxes will be paid by the top 1 percent of income earners. And no, they're not earning 39 percent of the income; more like 18 or 19 percent.

OK — we're going to make a slight diversion here to correct a misconception promoted by Democratic class warlords. This 39 percent of all federal income taxes is not, as they say, being paid by "the wealthiest 1 percent." The top 1 percent of income earners is paying it, and the top 1 percent of income earners does not necessarily correlate with the "wealthiest 1 percent" of Americans. Every year you have people in the middle-income groups who, through bonuses, buy-outs, the sale of assets, or some other economic windfall, see their income suddenly lurch — for that one year only — into the top 1 percent category. The next year they're right down there in the middle-income brackets again, wondering what in the hell happened to that nice bonus they got! Even though they were in that punishing top tax bracket for one year, and paying their share of the 39 percent, they are nowhere near becoming a member of the "Wealthiest 1 Percent" club.

Now — back to our figures.

Every year the liberals in congress propose ways to get more and more of their core constituents off the federal tax rolls. The favored methods now would be expanding the phony Earned Income Tax Credit (actually nothing more than an income redistribution program) or, even better, putting some brand new tax credits on the books. These tax credits — the childcare tax credit would be an example — usually phase out once a household passes the middle-income ranges. They're available, in other words, only to people who usually vote Democrat. The effect of these new credits is to wipe out whatever remaining tax liability there might be for the lower- and middle-income Democratic voters, thus shifting the total tax burden even more toward the higher-income ranges — evil rich people, you know, who have this disgusting propensity to vote for Republicans. As the paperback edition of this book is going to press, let us take a measure of just how the Democrats are progressing in their attempts to build their liberal, defeat-proof congress.

Right now the top 50 percent of income earners pays nearly 96 percent of all federal income taxes. The vast bulk of these taxes, well over 80 percent, are actually paid by the top 40 percent of income earners. With just a few more well-placed tax credits on the books, you would find it easier to find a liberal environmentalist watermelon (green on the outside, red on the inside) driving an SUV than to find someone in the lower 55 percent of income earners who actually pays federal income taxes.

Now, as I wrote earlier, let's imagine we have reached the point where nearly the entire burden for federal income taxes is being carried by the top 40 percent of income earners. Let's further imagine that around 55 or 60 percent of the income taxes collected by the Imperial Federal Government are paid right back out in the form of entitlements — with the bulk of these entitlements going to those with no federal income tax liability. Do you think, under these circumstances, that the ballot box will still be working for you?

That's where we're heading, folks. We're galloping toward the day (the figures would indicate that we're already there) where the liberals in Congress are able to use money seized from a minority of the voters to buy votes from the majority. With every year that passes, the actual tax-payers decrease in number while the tax-takers increase.

Somewhere in this "payers vs. takers" scenario we're going to reach a critical point of no return. This will be a point where those on the taking end will recognize their electoral dominance and will start groping for more and more. At that point, the liberals will have constructed their defeat-proof congress and the ballot box will have ceased to work, at least for the people paying the bills.

You can almost imagine the political campaign rhetoric now. There you are, making a relatively good living and enjoying the added benefits of various income supplements ("tax credits") from the government. Along comes an election and your Democratic candidate warns you that if you cast a vote for one of those evil conservatives out there you might lose some of your government income supplement checks and (gasp!) you might actually have to pay some income taxes! What are you going to do? You're going to vote Democrat, of course! It's a no-brainer!

THE BUSH TAX CUTS

This brings us to the Bush tax cut proposals. Here we are at a point where the government is taking a higher percentage of our gross domestic product in taxes than at any time in the history of the United States, save for one solitary year during World War II. The tax burden on the average American family has never been higher, and the Democrats are fighting tooth-and-nail to prevent any meaningful tax cut — especially if it means lowering rates for the evil top 1 percent.

Another side-trip here: Throughout the entire tax cut debate I got more than a little tired of hearing both sides talking about "giving money back." Tax cuts do not give any money back. Every single penny the Imperial Federal Government has collected stays with the government until the government spends it. A tax cut only means that the government will take less from the taxpayer in future years. It does not mean that the government is going to give anything back. I'm constantly amazed that all of our brilliant media-types can't get this one straight. You, on the other hand, are probably amazed that I'm amazed. I guess I should know better by now.

Anyway, there is one reason, and one reason only, that the Democrats fought the Bush tax cut so desperately. No, it wasn't because they were worried about funding Medicare or Social Security. The Democrats went on a holy war against the idea of a meaningful tax cut because they wanted to make sure that all that money would still be there when they regain control of the Congress. They will need that money to spend — to buy votes. They'll need that money to make sure that 1994 never happens again, that they never again lose the power they think is rightfully theirs in Washington.

The tax cut debate did illustrate, though, the success the left has gained thus far in its effort to build its defeat-proof entitlement majority. You probably remember seeing many polls that purported to show that the majority of Americans weren't really all that interested in a tax cut. The leftist media loved to trot this one out every chance it got. The premise was, I guess, that if the majority of people in this country didn't want a tax cut, then there shouldn't be a tax cut. Somehow, when presenting these poll results, they never seemed to mention that the majority of Americans don't have any significant federal tax liability anyway! It's no wonder they aren't worked up about the idea of a tax cut!

TAX CUTS FOR PEOPLE WHO DON'T PAY TAXES

When the liberals realized that they didn't have the numbers to stop a tax cut, they started working to turn it to their electoral advantage. The liberals had somewhat of a dilemma. They had been working for so many years to remove their core constituency from the tax rolls. Now they had nothing to offer these voters in the way of a tax cut! Only the higher-achievers were going to benefit, and those higher-achievers don't generally vote for Democrats!

Well, the solution was simple: Just get out there and boldly press for tax cuts for people who don't actually pay income taxes. Use the "fair" word. That usually does it! It's just not "fair" that so many people will get nothing from a tax cut! These people deserve their "fair share" of the budget surplus, too! So, any tax cut ought to include some pretty hefty checks for everyone! Even those who don't pay taxes!

Many columnists and commentators had quite a field day creating analogies to this liberal proposal. One of my favorites involved a cancelled baseball game. The team owners were going to refund the purchase price of all tickets until the local liberal politicians got into the game. It was unfair, they said, to refund the full ticket price to those who bought the expensive dugout level seats. Some of that money should be used to compensate those who were too poor to afford tickets to the game in the first place. The liberal mind at work.

To give a modicum of credibility to the demand for tax cuts for those who don't pay income taxes, the left came up with the payroll tax ploy. We were reminded that even if these people didn't pay income taxes, they were still paying Social Security and Medicare taxes and, therefore, they deserved a tax cut like everyone else!

Aha! Now we get a good look into the future plans of the left! Once they have succeeded in removing their core voters from the income tax rolls, they'll move toward giving them a free ride on Social Security and Medicare as well! Unlike income taxes, Social Security and Medicare taxes are specific fees paid in return for a specific benefit. You don't pay the fees, you're not eligible for the benefit. The liberals wish to change this. Their apparent goal is to shift the entire burden for the cost of Social Security and Medicare onto the high-achievers, along with the entire burden for federal income taxes.

The goal, then, is to create a class — a majority class — of government-dependent voters who have but one civic duty. That duty is not to live a life of responsibility so as not to become a burden on the state or their neighbors. That goal is simply to show up at the polls when directed to do so and make sure that their vote is cast for their liberal political benefactors. This, my friends, is a task that they will be only too happy to perform. The achievers — the minority — will be voting to keep the money they earn. The rest will be voting to take it.

Maybe it's time to plan an escape route. Does anyone know where Galt's Gulch is?